To Pauline and Jim

Happy reading

Steve

THE FINANCIAL TIMES

HANDBOOK OF FINANCIAL MANAGEMENT

THE FINANCIAL TIMES

HANDBOOK OF FINANCIAL MANAGEMENT

Steve Robinson

FT
PITMAN
PUBLISHING

PITMAN PUBLISHING
128 Long Acre, London WC2E 9AN

A Division of Longman Group Limited

First published in Great Britain 1995

British Library Cataloguing in Publication Data
A CIP catalogue record for this book can be obtained from the British Library.

ISBN 0 273 60338 8

3 5 7 9 10 8 6 4

Typeset by Northern Phototypesetting Co. Ltd, Bolton
Printed and bound in Great Britain by
Bell & Bain Ltd, Glasgow

*The Publishers' policy is to use paper manufactured
from sustainable forests.*

CONTENTS

PREFACE

The main aim of this book is to remove the mystery that surrounds the subject of finance. I have therefore made every effort to ensure that it is interesting, enjoyable and relevant. The stages that you will go through during the course of reading the book will possibly look like this:

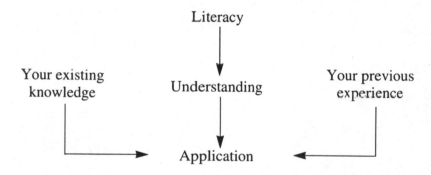

A comprehensive text for all the subject headings is not provided; many excellent, detailed texts already exist and others will appear in the future. However, I hope this will provide you with the fundamental knowledge and enthusiasm needed in order to search for them.

Many people have supported me in the writing of this book. To single out any one, or even a few, would be unfair to the others. To all of you I offer my sincere thanks and gratitude.

Steve Robinson 1995

INTRODUCTION

SETTING THE SCENE

This book has been written primarily for the UK market, although attempts have been made to incorporate as illustrations non-UK companies and accounting practices. It would not be practical to attempt to cover language equivalents in every case, but as many US books are used worldwide in the study of finance some common principal terms are given below.

UK	US
Limited (Ltd)	Incorporated (Inc)
Ordinary shares	Common stock
Company	Corporation
Stock	Inventory
Debtors	Receivable
Creditors	Payable

THE BEGINNING

I want to start this book with an easy-to-read introduction to the terms associated with companies and the way their finances are managed.

THE BIRTH AND EARLY LIFE OF A COMPANY

A company is a separate entity in law from the owners, directors or employees and should be conceived as a vehicle for developing a business idea. The use of a suffix such as private limited, public limited, sarl inc, GmbH or Pty indicates that the liability of the owners of the *company* is limited to the amount of money they have actually paid or agreed to pay for their *shares* which are the evidence of ownership. How many shares and their initial value are two of the first financial decisions made by a company. This shapes its ownership structure and can determine the rate of growth and size of the company in the future.

The very first financial decision should emerge from the business plan, which identified the long and short term funding needs. Further chapters of this book discuss criteria for selecting funding sources, but as borrowing is difficult or even impossible in some countries for a new business with no track record and possibly an untried idea, let's assume that the owners have got to put some of their own (or personally borrowed) cash into the company. There are no fixed criteria for the amount of the *nominal value* or specified issue amount of a share.

Illustration

A company has decided to raise £1,000,000 by issuing shares. It can issue two shares with a nominal value of £500,000 each but that would limit the number of shareholders to two and restrict the potential shareholder market to those willing and able to invest £500,000. It would be more practical to have a million shares of £1 each or a greater number of even smaller units.

The most common UK value is 25p, which, in our example, would give four million shares. In the US 25¢ is common, while in Japan nominal values are very much higher, e.g. NTT (the Japanese Telecommunications utility). The value of the company, or *market capitalisation*, will be £1m. If we go ahead and sell (issue) the shares to investors they become *shareholders,* owning a part of the company. In the UK, companies cannot sell more new shares for cash without first offering them to existing shareholders in proportion to the number of shares which they already own – a *rights* issue. Thus the ownership structure can be determined at the outset. If the shareholder cannot keep buying the new shares to which he has a right, known as a *cash call*, his holding will *dilute,* going down as a percentage although the same number of shares will be held.

The company will probably want to make *capital investment*, spending cash now for future returns, and acquire in the process *fixed assets*, which are items of value bought by the company for its own use. Some of these assets will be *tangible* – real physical items such as buildings, machinery and equipment – some will be *intangible* – less physically identifiable things such as brands, information systems and distribution agreements. As trading starts, the company will accumulate *current assets*, which are items of value acquired day by day such as stocks of goods for resale or to be used in a manufacturing process.

Where products or services are sold but payment is not received *debtors* are created. When they pay, *cash* is received – the most liquid of all current assets. This short term investment in the business is often partly financed by *supplier creditors*, who are willing to wait for payment for their goods or services that we have bought. Frequently, a *bank overdraft* acts as a short term source of cash, but as this is often repayable at short notice there should be a strategy for financial emergencies.

After a period of trading, usually a year initially, the *financial accounts* or profit and loss cash flow and balance sheet are produced. They are of interest to:

- **shareholders,** as they own the company and are entitled to be informed of the financial position
- **tax authorities,** so they may collect taxes based on the rules set by the Governments
- **lenders,** who wish to evaluate the security of their investment
- **suppliers,** who are vulnerable as they provide goods based only on a promise to pay in the future
- **employees,** who may make an attempt to assess the security of their jobs
- **competitors** trying to uncover something to help their own business
- **investors in general** to help them in their continual searches for a home for cash.

If there is a profit the shareholders may well expect a *dividend* or return on their investment. The profit figure relevant here is *profit attributable to ordinary shareholders,* better known as *earnings*. If all of this figure were distributed as dividend the *dividend payout ratio* would be 100 per cent and the *retained profit*, left in the business for re-investment, would be zero. Shareholders usually want their dividends in cash, and cash is what the company needs to invest in the future – more of this later.

Thus a company is born and completes its first year. As the business grows there will be a need for further investment. There are three sources for this – the shareholders, the lenders and profits retained rather than paid as dividends. Decisions need also to be made about the long and short term financial management of the business. Illustrations of how these decisions are reached have been described in the financial case histories of 11 companies which appear at the end of the book.

1

MEASURING THE PERFORMANCE OF A BUSINESS

CHAPTER OBJECTIVES
- To aid understanding of the meaning and usefulness of financial information
- To introduce comprehensive financial analysis techniques
- To identify key performance measures
- To relate relevant performance measures to specific business situations

The assessment of business performance in financial terms is demanded by investors, lenders, supplier creditors, employees, tax authorities, Government agencies and the information providers that serve them. Fortunately, most business is carried out by limited liability companies which have to disclose financial data for statutory purposes. Where a company is quoted on a stock exchange or market much more information is available on its performance because regulations demand a higher level of disclosure to protect investors. Most large UK companies have a full listing, which means that more than 25 per cent of their ordinary (voting) shares are held by the investing 'public', which includes professional investors responsible for investing other people's money, known collectively as the institutions.

WHERE DO WE START?

Reading financial reports can be pure pleasure to some, but a daunting and intimidating task to the majority. There is a lot of detailed information but it is divided into three parts:

- profit or income statement
- cash flow statement
- position statement or balance sheet.

The profit statement or income statement

This provides the profitability picture for the *whole* business. More detailed breakdowns are provided in the reviews of the Chief Executive and operating company executives. Information disclosure requirements are becoming more exacting. An example of this in the UK recently has been the introduction of tighter financial reporting standards, by the newly formed Accounting Standards Board who have replaced earlier Statements of Standard Accounting Practice (SSAPs) with new Financial Reporting Standards (FRSs) which requires sales and profits divided into discontinued, continuing and acquired businesses to be declared in the main statement, not in small-print notes. Profit is derived from sales and costs, producing margins. Scope for cost reduction could be identified from comparing margins across the product range and by comparison with competitors.

Cash flow statement

This provides an analysis of cash movements:

Inputs

- generated by the business
- supplied by owners
- supplied by lenders
- realised from asset disposals and divestments

Outputs

- paid in dividends
- paid in interest
- invested in assets and acquisitions.

Position statement or balance sheet

This provides an overview of the financial state of the business:

BALANCE SHEET WINDOW

	FUNDING	INVESTING
LONG TERM	Share capital Retained profits Loans	Fixed tangible assets Intangible assets Strategic investments
SHORT TERM	Bank overdraft Supplier creditors Third party, e.g. sales taxes	Stock Debtors Cash

THE NEXT STEPS – DIGGING DEEPER

- **Read the accounting policies.** This is essentially a major part of the rules as applied by this specific business. Close similarity or adjustment is needed for competitor comparisons.
- **Make comprehensive use of the notes.** They aid understanding by breaking down totals, enabling more detailed analysis, and by explaining situations and changes.
- **Segmental analysis.** Look for sales profits and capital employed analysed by business sector and geographical area. This often pinpoints key profit generators and highlights where investments are at risk.
- **Study the five year history.** This helps to provide a longer term historic perspective, although it can be massively distorted by acquisitions or divestments.
- **Ownership.** Who owns the business? In the UK holders of more than 3 per cent of ordinary voting shares have to make their holding

public and the company has to list these holders in the annual report. Large institutional holders can give stability but perhaps leave the business vulnerable to the views of a small number of individuals (see the London Weekend Television case). In contrast, a large entrepreneurial holding can be a limiting factor on growth but it can mean that someone has a great deal of money to lose if things go wrong – and a powerful incentive to ensure they do not.

- **Capital investment.** Business carries on into the future. In most situations this requires investment to:
  - replace fixed assets to protect profitability
  - purchase additional fixed assets to generate extra profit
  - research and develop new products and services
  - develop and implement marketing and sales strategies
  - meet the information technology needs
  - finance growth by acquisition
  - develop our human resources.

BEYOND HISTORIC FINANCIAL DATA

The underlying purpose of analysing historic financial data is to predict future performance. Many useful sources of data such as market forecasts and pay agreements exist outside of financial reports. The successful interpretation of the interaction between environmental factors and the specific situation of the company is the key to predicting future performance. Four aspects of the business are likely to have major financial implications for the future:

- **People.** Often the key strength of the business, they need paying regularly, often regardless of the state of the business. They have to be well compensated when they are no longer needed and sometimes provided for in the future via pension funding. The more people there are in the business, the greater the impact on cash now and in the future. The notes to the accounts will contain an analysis of employee numbers.
- **Borrowing facilities.** The balance sheet gives details of actual current borrowings, but an important additional component is the availability of further borrowings, both committed and

uncommitted. Large numbers here are a measure of confidence by lenders and a measure of the attitude to risk adopted by the board.

- **Fixed asset investment.** Often the largest part of fixed asset investment is property. There are two scenarios which can result from ownership – benefit in the form of a capital gain or a penalty because of capital losses and/or maintenance or refurbishment type obligations. The major write-downs seen in the UK recently are an indication of current market conditions. Retail property has been particularly badly affected. Examples in 1994 include J. Sainsbury plc which has had to write down the value of its UK properties by £341.5m and adjust its policy to reflect changing conditions. (Also see Queens Moat Houses case.)
- **Environmental impact.** It is pretty certain that if the activities of a business are having an adverse impact on the environment, then some time in the future that business will have to pay. If the burden is too great the value of share investment will be zero, and in any event the returns will be affected over time. Either way, the shareholders ultimately will suffer in financial terms.

MEASURING FINANCIAL PERFORMANCE – 'THE JIGSAW'

Measuring the financial performance of a business is like doing a jigsaw. The more pieces you can link together the better the picture and the more meaningful. These are the main components contributing towards the assessment.

The Jigsaw – accounting measures information sources (Figure 1.1)

Cash flow – contained in the cash flow statement.

Approach:

- identify major inflows and outflows
- isolate non-recurrent items.

Calculate:

- *'Operating' cash flow* – cash generated after paying day to day expenses

Accounting measures

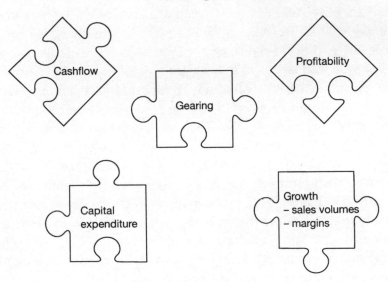

Market measures

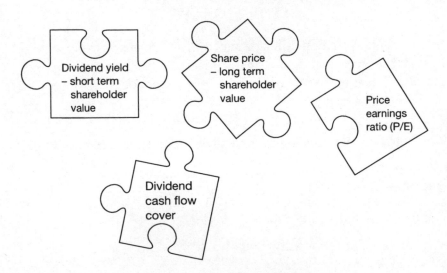

Figure 1.1

- *'Post financing'* cash flow – taking out the cash costs of funding the company-interest and dividend
- *'Post capital expenditure' cash flow* – taking out the necessary investment for the future to protect and maintain the current earning potential of the business
- *'Free' cash flow* – the cash available for investment in the long term growth of the business after all of the above payments.

Profitability – contained in the profit or income statement.

Approach:

- identify major profit contributors – concentrating on the continuing business – by geographic area, product group and market sector
- relate investment and return in as many as possible of the analyses above
- isolate non-recurrent profits and losses and establish repeatable earnings (profit after tax, interest and minorities).

Gearing – contained in the balance sheet or position statement.

Approach:

- identify the relationship between 'owner investment' and long term borrowing
- refine the analysis to show the effect of including/excluding intangible assets, such as brands, the impact of including off balance sheet finance, redefining the boundaries of debt and equity and of the length of the 'long' term.

Growth – available in the profit statement and the balance sheet.

- Volume and margin growth will be found in the profit statement. It is important to look at both, as the key is often the interaction of the two as seen in the operating profit figure.
- A more general overview can be obtained from the balance sheet. Areas to be looked for are growth of fixed assets (both by acquisition and valuation), and levels of current assets and current liabilities. Growth in any one of these can be a sign of weakness because scarce cash has been committed. Strength does not come simply from the

acquisition of assets but also from employing them in order to generate cash returns in excess of their financing cost.

Capital expenditure – in total, the cash flow statement, itemised between categories of the fixed asset schedule in the notes to the balance sheets.

Approach:

- compare the expenditure by category with the amount of depreciation in the fixed assets schedule in the balance sheet notes. This will give an indication of whether it can be maintained. A study of the relevant accounting policies will be necessary to reach a judgement
- the proportion of capital expenditure being generated by the 'post financing' cash flow is a good indication of the ability of the business to fund growth without borrowing or shareholder investment.

An overview of assessing business performance is provided in Figure 1.2. The core is the *present* but the *past* plays a part and predicting the *future* is the ultimate purpose. *Comparisons* are an important part in determining *financial strength* which ensures *investment returns* leading to enhancing *shareholder value*.

The Jigsaw – market measures information sources (Figure 1.1)

Shareholder value

This is the combined return from dividend income and capital growth in share value attributable to the owners of the company. (See Chapter 9 for more detail.) Dividend income is determined by the directors of the company but has to be approved by the shareholders. Although the actual dividend figure is shown in the financial report it is more meaningful to relate it to the current share price in the market and establish the dividend yield. That is the return being achieved today in relation to the 'opportunity cost' – the amount the share could be sold for and the potential investment yield from that amount. Share price is only provided in financial reports to enable capital taxes to be determined. Markets are volatile and prices change frequently and sometimes dramatically. The price is the judgement of the market about the future,

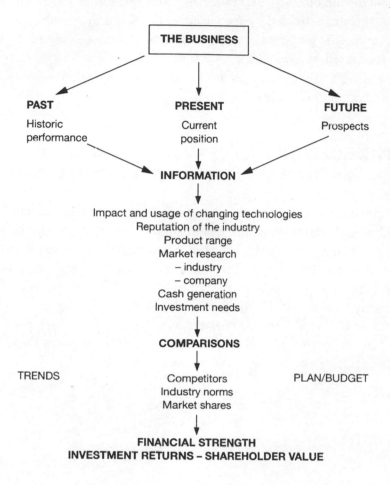

ASSESSING BUSINESS PERFORMANCE OVER TIME

THE BUSINESS

PAST
Historic
performance

PRESENT
Current
position

FUTURE
Prospects

INFORMATION

Impact and usage of changing technologies
Reputation of the industry
Product range
Market research
– industry
– company
Cash generation
Investment needs

COMPARISONS

TRENDS

Competitors
Industry norms
Market shares

PLAN/BUDGET

FINANCIAL STRENGTH
INVESTMENT RETURNS – SHAREHOLDER VALUE

Figure 1.2

not the past, and is becoming more focused on cash generation, as this is how dividends are paid.

Dividend cash flow cover

Dividends are paid mainly in cash. A measure of how safe this dividend could be is how many times the dividend could be paid out of the free cash flow.

Price earnings (P/E) ratio

This is the relationship, expressed as a multiple, of the current market price of a share divided by the earnings per share. It is widely quoted for comparison purposes in the financial newspapers. A high P/E ratio can be caused by two factors – a high share price or a low earnings figure. Essentially it comes down to the same conclusion – the market has a very optimistic view.

THE ROLE OF RATIOS IN ASSESSING BUSINESS PERFORMANCE – 'THE RULE OF FIVES'

Comprehensive analysis of business performance must include both absolute and relationship numbers to enable comparison with competitors and industry standards. The choice of which numbers to use to provide insights into the performance of a specific company is an individual one. The greater the knowledge of the operations of the company, the better the quality of the selection of key ratios. The objective of Table 1.1 is to provide five key areas in which performance can be evaluated and to select the two most important numbers within each area to give ten performance indicators.

Table 1.1

Performance indicator	Calculation	Information source
	Profitability	
Return on sales	Earnings: sales	Profit statement
Return on capital employed	Earnings: total capital employed	Profit statement and position statement
	Cash Management	
Cash flow cover	Operating cash flow Dividend and interest payments	Cash flow statement
Free cash flow	Cash available for investment in the longer term growth of business	Cash flow statement
	Operational Control	
Return on managed assets	Earnings: specific capital employed in a business unit	Segmental analyses
	Capital structure	
Gearing	Debt: equity	Position statement
Investment for the future	Cash spent	Cash flow statement
	Investment Return	
Dividend yield	Most recent year dividend payment: share price	Cash flow statement and financial press
Dividend cash flow	Actual total cash dividend payment	Cash flow statement

2

FINANCING THE BUSINESS

CHAPTER OBJECTIVES
- To describe the long term sources of funds available to businesses
- To analyse the process for selecting from the available sources
- To provide a checklist of factors to help in making the decisions
- To examine the process of selling shares to the public
- To evaluate the factors influencing the dividend decision
- To identify the key influences in borrowing arrangements
- To describe the process of rating potential borrowers

The most fundamental and certainly the earliest strategic financial management decision is how to finance the business. At the initial stages in the life of an independent business the options may be limited.

New businesses are notoriously risky because there is no track record to support either a case for permanent investment or for long term borrowing. A case for permanent investment in the form of shares would need to provide hope of growth in value over the long term with some cash returns in the short term. The borrowing case is different, as the need to pay cash interest regularly is paramount. Lenders lose patience quickly and breaches of covenants give them considerable extra power – voting rights or even outright ownership of specific assets. If the lender is a bank then the loan becomes classified as 'non-performing' and its auditors put pressure on to take a bad debt write-off. Such pressure affects the financing decision and the way the business is managed (see Euro-Disney case).

TIME SCALES FOR FUNDING

The fundamental principle is to match source with use. Long term finance is usually for acquisition, asset purchase or organic business development. As these activities rarely generate cash in the short term, it is important to obtain long term funding to avoid taking decisions aimed only at maximising profit in the short term as this often damages profit potential for the future. Typical situations would be reducing an advertising and promotion campaign having already spent heavily on developing the product, or cutting back on maintenance, which often leads to significantly higher future costs.

LONG TERM FUNDING

The two sources of long term funding to a business are *debt* (borrowing) and *equity* (ownership).

DEBT *v.* EQUITY

Decision criteria:
- permanence
- control or dilution
- cost to borrower

Permanence

When a share has been sold by a company it is available on the open market for ever. There are two relatively minor exceptions:

- share buy-back – which is voluntary on the part of the seller, e.g. Boots plc announcement November 1994.
- minority buy-out. In the case of an acquisition where 90 per cent of the target's shareholders have accepted, the acquiror can purchase the remaining shares. There is a small catch: the price must be the highest paid by the acquiror within the last 18 months.

Control or dilution

There are critical points in ownership levels which influence the amount of shares that can be issued. Shareholder approval must be obtained for pre-emption, and individual holders may be unwilling to see their stake reduced.

Cost to borrower

The interest paid on debt is tax-deductible, unlike dividend payments, which are treated as a distribution of profit. The after-tax cost of borrowing can often provide cheaper finance without the implications of ownership.

EQUITY

Equity funding is selling parts or shares in the company to investors. The majority of these investors will be financial institutions such as pension funds, insurance companies and unit trusts who aim to achieve a balance of current income and long term growth commensurate with minimising the risk. Their influence in financial markets is enormous. In the UK their equity holdings amount to 75 per cent of the total value of the market.

Types of equity shares

Table 2.1   Share characteristics

	Ordinary	*Preference*	*Convertible**
Voting	Yes	No	No
Dividend	Variable	Fixed	Fixed and low
Liquidation ranking	3rd	2nd	1st
Most likely to benefit if all goes well	1st	3rd	2nd

* Convertibles will take the same characteristics as ordinary shares immediately on conversion.

Ordinary shares are the main permanent risk capital of the company. The shareholders will be the main beneficiaries of the success of the business, and the main losers if it fails. They are invariably the only sharer with voting powers and have the permanent 'right' to maintain their proportion of the business by buying new shares offered to them as a rights issue. Their voting powers mean they must approve any reduction in their rights – known as pre-emption in the UK. It is normal to ask shareholders to waive part of these. As an illustration Guinness plc in 1994 asked for the authority to issue up to 100 million shares for the purposes of option schemes or to make acquisitions. This flexibility is useful in the acquisition process. The amount is around 5 per cent of the issued ordinary share capital, which is the guide maximum figure put forward by one of the institutional shareholder groups, the Association of British Insurers.

It is normal again in the UK to seek authority to enable the company to use company resources to repurchase its own ordinary shares. The maximum level, within institutional investor guidelines, is 10 per cent of the issued share capital, and Guinness plc in 1994 obtained approval to buy up to 200 million shares. The purpose of such action could be to:

- enhance earnings per share
- support the share price by building confidence
- defend against a predatory bid.

Both of these authorities remain in place for around a year, when they must be confirmed by the shareholders. More routine matters that they have to approve at the annual general meeting are:

- the accounts
- the level of dividend
- the re-appointment of auditors
- the election of directors.

Shareholders in the UK rarely attend company meetings. They appear to go only when there has been some scandal such as when the Burton Group share option scheme for directors came up for approval in early 1987. The scheme would have provided considerable benefits to the Board then under the chairmanship of Ralph Halpern. At the time there were suggestions of impropriety with a *Sun* newspaper page 3 model.

Preference shares are a way for a company to raise permanent capital at a fixed rate of interest. As preference shareholders have no voting powers they do not affect the control or ownership of the company. A disadvantage can be a relatively high interest rate if rates have fallen generally in the market. If the shares are *redeemable* then the company can exercise its right to buy them back. In some cases, if there is a default on payment of interest the preference shareholders get some voting rights to enable them to protect their position (see the Saatchi and Saatchi case). Preference shares count as equity on the balance sheet, although in other respects they are identical to debt.

Illustration

New Issues. The UK market was very active in 1994 with nearly 150 new companies coming to the market in the first half of the year. They have raised £7.5bn, and their initial market value has added around £13bn to the total market of £700bn. If non-UK companies listed and traded are added, this figure jumps by nearly £3,000bn. Table 2.2 traces the activity up to July 1994.

Table 2.2

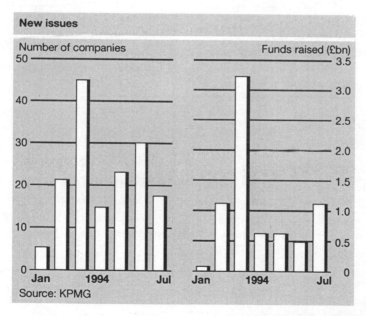

Source: KPMG

Convertibles are a half-way house between equity and debt. They start life with debt characteristics. Convertible preference shares carry a fixed *coupon* or interest rate with conversion conditions to ordinary shares and dates specified when they are issued.

Illustration

Today's ordinary share price (mid-1994)   £4.00
Issue price of convertible preference share   £4.00
Interest payment 2 per cent per annum
Share may be exchanged for cash during the period mid-1998 to end 1999, after which it becomes a low-interest debt.

Alternatively

One convertible preference share can be exchanged for one ordinary share to rank equally with all other ordinary shares in issue. The merits for the company and the investor are shown in Table 2.3:

Table 2.3   What makes convertibles work?

For the company	For the investor
Low interest finance	Some (small) interim return
Relatively long term	Finite time commitment
Potentially never repayable	Certainty of capital return
More shareholders	Potential for up-side gain
– but a larger profit 'cake' to share	

The investor has to make a judgement on the potential share price in mid-1998 onwards. If this offer is not attractive enough to investors the company has several ways to improve its appeal (see Table 2.4). The decision would be made depending on company needs.

Table 2.4   Structuring a convertible issue to ensure success

Component	Drawback to company
Lower issue price	Less cash raised initially
Higher interest rate	Higher cash interest cost for the
Earlier repayment/conversion	next five years
option date	Cash available for a shorter term
Pay a special dividend on conversion	period; increases pressure on
	short-term performance
	Higher cash outlay *but* payable in
	five years' time

THE PROCESS OF ISSUING SHARES

Ordinary shares, or common stock, are the principal risk capital permanently invested in the business. Only in rare circumstances does the company buy back ordinary shares; Boots plc announced in November 1994 its intention to spend £500m on a share buy-back programme). The shareholder has to look to a secondary market such as the London Stock Exchange to find a buyer when he wishes to sell. Share buy-back has been common in the US for some years, where it has been used by companies to buy shares held by corporate raiders such as T. Boone Pickens and Carl Icahn. They were perceived as a threat to the existing management, who used the company's cash (or their borrowing facilities) to buy back and cancel shares, so eliminating the influence of a powerful unwanted minority.

The Companies Act 1985 in the UK allowed companies to repurchase their own shares, but a limit was set of 10 per cent of the issued shares in any one year and then only after shareholder approval. The powerful Institutional Investors Committee has introduced a tighter non-statutory control. A theoretical justification for a company re-purchasing its own shares was to enhance earnings per share and reduce future dividend payments. In practice this must be compared with the loss of interest income or interest cost if cash was borrowed.

The first time a company seeks to have its shares traded publicly is known as 'going public' or, more commonly, 'flotation'. In the US this is known as an Initial Public Offering (IPO). There are two ways of coming to the market:

- **an offer for sale** is where either the company sells more shares to raise cash or where existing investors sell some or all of their holdings, or a combination of both (see Field Group plc case)
- **an introduction,** where the company raises no new money and none of the existing shareholders sell. This can only work where there are a considerable number of existing shareholders and enough volume for regular trading. The normal purpose of an introduction is to enable trading to take place on another exchange, usually known as a 'secondary listing'. Many UK companies have this facility in the US, e.g. Hanson.

There is no formula for deciding whether to come to the market with an offer for sale or an introduction. It depends on the motives for seeking the listing.

SELLING SHARES TO THE PUBLIC

Reasons for listing – 'going public'

- For backers to realise some or all of their investment.
- For directors and senior managers to realise cash from their holdings.
- To create a market for the shares both in the short and long terms.
- To provide access to a wider investor community.

Requirements for listing

- **Accounts.** Three years published.
- **Working capital.** Company must have adequate working capital for at least the next 12 months.
- **Controlling shareholder.** Where a holder has more than 30 per cent of the votes, directors must have independent power to make decisions.
- **Minimum market value of shares.** £700,000.
- **Minimum distribution.** More than 25 per cent of each class of share must be available to the public. This is to ensure that there is potentially an adequate supply of shares to satisfy demand and avoid the very large swings which can occur in a 'thin' market.

Publish a prospectus

This document is the selling document for the shares to prospective buyers. It contains a mass of detail, but the main components are:

- background to the company and the industry
- directors, management and professional advisers
- historic financial statements
- forecast profits and dividends
- details of the share capital structure
- specification of the indebtedness, guarantees and commitments.

The role of advisers

Merchant Bank

- Main role – active marketing of the idea
- Frequently an existing investor
- Often acts as the underwriter.

Broker

- Researching likely demand for the issue
- Pricing the issue
- Stock Exchange liaison
- Market making.

Reporting accountants

- Producing financial position statements
- Commenting on internal controls systems and management information.

Lawyers

- Dual roles – company and shareholders.

Financial PR consultants

- Publicity arrangements
- Links with the press.

RIGHTS ISSUES

After the first share issue has taken place in the UK, the principle of pre-emption comes into play, which gives shareholders the right to maintain the proportion of shares they hold in the company.

If a company decides that the best option at this time for raising funds is to sell shares, one of the criteria in making this decision will have been the current market price of the share. To be successful and attract shareholders to 'take up their rights' the shares have to be offered at a discount, typically 15 per cent, to the current market price. If the current market price is low then the company will not raise as much cash. Often a low share price will have left shareholders relatively unhappy and maybe unwilling to invest any more cash. However, a share price is much more likely to rise from a low base. In contrast, a high share price realises more money for the company, is often eagerly received by a contented audience, but will have a hard time living up to ever-increasing expectations. Another drawback is the frequency with which shareholders can be approached. Conventional wisdom indicates this period to be perhaps no more than every three years (see Saatchi and Saatchi case).

SCRIP ISSUES

Exceptions have occurred. Saatchi and Saatchi plc, the global advertising agency, pursued a vigorous acquisition policy in the mid-to-late 1980s, coming successfully to shareholders for large sums of cash in a variety of forms in consecutive years when mounting interest payments and poor business performance hit the share price . Those shareholders who retained their holdings faced decimating losses in later years. Rights issues are often confused with scrip, bonus or capitalisation issues. The distinction is very clear. Scrip issues do not raise any cash for the company. They are merely book entries converting reserves into issued share capital. Any category of reserve such as retained profit, share premium or revaluation surplus can be transferred in this way. It has absolutely no effect on the assets of the business, it just divides the company into more (each one smaller) parts or shares.

SHARE SPLITS

A similar confusion exists with share splits. These are common in the UK. In 1991 both Glaxo and Guinness split their shares. In the case of Guinness one 50p share was divided into two 25p shares. The direct effect on the shareholder and the company was only to double the number of shares. In this case, because the announcement was made at the same time as an encouraging trading statement the market price of two new shares exceeded one old one – but it was the information content that triggered the rise.

The logic behind a share split is difficult to support. The contention is that shares are more marketable to private investors at lower prices. Many new public offers are in the £2–£3 range. Comparison with Continental companies – Nestlé at £600 per share, for example – indicates a British trait. Taking the comparison further to Japan with Japan Tobacco at £9,400 for each share is bewildering. Perhaps it is just an example of British modesty. In April 1994 the Reuters four for one split was defended by its spokesman thus, 'We were the only stock trading above £20 (in the FTSE 100) and that made us an exception'. The Guinness split occurred when the share price was around £11, while figures of around £14–£16 are often quoted as being a maximum to stimulate a split.

THE DIVIDEND DECISION

Dividends, by providing regular income in the short term, are one of the two ways of rewarding shareholders. The other is to manage the business in such a way that the capital value of the investment is maximised. This implies making a judgement between retaining cash for investment and distributing it in the form of dividends.

Factors influencing the dividend decision

- Information content – last year's payment
- Legality
- Ability to pay the cash
- Market expectations
- Alternative investment opportunities
- Restrictive covenants
- Taxation
- Ownership expectations

Information content – last year's payment

The most important determinant is the amount of dividend paid last year. Any decision is conveying information to the investment community and is open to misinterpretation (see Table 2.5); good financial communication to accompany the announcement, therefore, is essential.

Table 2.5

Amount of dividend payable	Possible interpretations
Reduction	Bad year: cannot afford to pay or using cash for investment
No change	Marginal performance: struggling to maintain payment or no confidence in the future of correct balance achieved
Increase	Good year: under-investing, may be fine *this* year but can it continue or will long term performance be affected by a failure to adequately re-invest?

Legality

Statutory restrictions exist to limit the amount of dividend payable to broadly the amount of accounting profit, including retained profit from previous years' trading. This is not normally a problem, but the Queens Moat Houses (see case) illustrates that difficulties can arise. At the time of writing, the company is under investigation for allegedly paying unlawful dividends in 1991, 1992 and 1993. The rules exist to protect creditors and investors in the normal operation of a business but the more common problem is finding the cash to make the payments.

Ability to pay the cash

Dividends are paid mainly in cash. Although an increased number of companies offer a 'scrip' dividend alternative – receiving a number of new shares equivalent to the dividend payment – only about 2 per cent take up this option. Companies are naturally keen to conserve their cash and continue to encourage the scrip alternative. There was a surge of scrip dividend offers during 1993, following fiscal changes. Companies with a particular type of tax 'loss' (unrelieved Advance Corporation Tax – ACT) in the UK offered scrip dividends 50 per cent higher than cash payments. This prompted further fiscal changes and the introduction of another alternative, FIDS (Foreign Income Dividends), which will be highly tax efficient for those UK companies that make a substantial part of their profits overseas.

Market expectations

The views of the market – regularly made public in the form of analysts' forecasts – cannot be ignored. The London International Group (see case) went to a great deal of trouble to change analysts' views, although not by the appropriate methods. Good financial communication will ensure that the briefings are accurate and forecasts reflect the reality of current business performance.

Alternative investment opportunities

One of the consequences of paying cash dividends is an inevitable reduction in cash available for re-investment in any form in the business. Areas affected could be:

- long term capital expenditure (capex) for business development
- shorter term capex for profit maintenance projects
- current asset investment.

Restrictive covenants

Lenders often impose restrictions on how companies manage their business, particularly where there is an impact on the cash. A common control is to limit the amount of dividend in some way, for example:

- as a percentage of the profit for the year
- capped at a cash limit
- restricted to a maximum percentage increase on the previous year.

Taxation

In the UK the payment of dividends is not a tax deductible expense. In fact paying a dividend attracts an early payment – Advance Corporation Tax (ACT) – related to the amount of dividend. In the past it has been equivalent to the standard income tax rate. This payment can be deducted from the company tax due at a later stage, termed mainstream Corporation Tax. This makes an impact on the company in two ways:

- cash outflow increases as the cash dividend is increased
- the company needs to be making a taxable profit to recover the ACT against the mainstream Corporation Tax.

Ownership expectations

Financial institutions need some cash flow to enable them to meet their commitments and generally only invest in companies that pay a dividend. There is some UK investor protection legislation which restricts investment in companies not paying a dividend. Some other shareholders may well be happy to receive low or even no dividend, content for the cash to be reinvested in the business. There is a logic in a company retaining £1 for investment rather than giving the same amount to the shareholder, who will receive only perhaps 75p, with income tax of 25p deducted.

Table 2.6   Contrasting dividend policies

	Cash cost of dividend (in £million)			
	1990	**1991**	**1992**	**1993**
BOOKER	32	43	44	46
GUINNESS	162	193	221	244
BT	769	859	917	999
	Dividend as a % of operating cash flow			
BOOKER	26%	26%	42%	30%
GUINNESS	21%	23%	25%	26%
BT	4%	15%	18%	19%
	Dividend as a % of net income			
BOOKER	41%	107%	112%	77%
GUINNESS	30%	35%	45%	60%
BT	39%	43%	79%	59%

Dividend data of three companies has been produced in the Table 2.6:

- Booker is involved in three core business areas – food wholesaling,

food processing and agribusiness – and 85 per cent of its turnover is
in the UK
- Guinness is an international drinks company focused on beer and
spirits with 80 per cent of its turnover outside the UK
- British Telecommunications is the main supplier of telecommunications services in the UK. It has a market share of almost 90 per cent
and almost all of its turnover is in the UK.

The contrasting dividend policies from the three companies have significant similarities and differences:

Similarities:

- They have all increased in all three years both in cash cost and as a
percentage of operating cash flow.

Differences:

- As a proportion of net income Booker has accepted the need to pay
more (cash) dividend than the company has earned (profit),
rectifying the situation in 1993 from improved performance.
- Guinness has increased its dividend payment at a more rapid rate
than profit.
- BT has made large profit write-offs, particularly in 1992, which has
distorted the picture.

The market interprets this and other information in arriving at a judgement on price. The dividend paid, as a percentage of the current market
price, is the dividend yield. If short term income is the key objective of
investment, Booker is the first choice:

Current dividend yield	
Booker	6.4 %
Guinness	3.5 %
BT	5.6 %

THE US MARKET

The period 1988–1993 has seen a great increase in UK companies
seeking a listing in the US. There are two main exchanges. The larger
companies tend to go for the New York Stock Exchange, the smaller

ones choose National Association of Security Dealers Automated Quotation System (NASDAQ). NASDAQ is designed for smaller companies as the size criteria for income and number of shareholders are lower. Both are regulated by the Securities Exchange Commission and insist on US Accounting Policies (GAAP) being applied in the preparation of financial statements. This was a barrier preventing any German companies from being quoted on any US Exchange until 1993. Mercedes-Benz became the first company to agree to adopt GAAP. Under German rules the profit for 1992 was US$104m. When GAAP was applied this became a loss of US$586m.

American investors have an appetite for UK shares, and companies quoted include Hanson, Glaxo, Bass and Tate & Lyle. The shares are traded in ADR (American Depository Receipt) form – for example, Saatchi ADRs represent three ordinary shares, Bass ADRs represent two ordinary shares. The way the system operates is that the ADR is held by a bank and it is the 'Receipt' that is traded, thus avoiding the need to change the holder's name on the share register. A recent figure from the Bank of New York put the total UK value of ADRs at $52bn. All buying, selling and dividend payments are in US dollars.

Large US investors such as Fidelity and Berkshire Hathaway, the fund headed by the legendary Warren Buffet*, have sufficient international experience to invest in a local market and would probably hold ADRs. Smaller institutions such as mutual funds (unit trusts) would prefer to invest and receive income in dollars, so the ADR is an ideal form.

Retail investors are more interested in UK shares if they have a profile in the US with their businesses, products and services. They tend to be very understanding about the business and have more interest in strong cash flows than asset values and gearing levels.

---

*Warren Buffet is the American billionaire who, from his home base in Omaha, Nebraska, has established one of the most successful mutual funds (similar to unit trusts) ever. He was responsible for rebuilding Saloman Brothers' image following their admission to cheating the US Government in the period up to 1991 by effectively rigging the auctions of US Government stocks and bonds. As a director and major investor he moved rapidly dismissing the Chief Executive Officer and taking a double page spread advertisement in the Wall Street Journal to apologise for their mistakes. The result was that confidence returned and crucially the US Government agreed to continue to deal with the company. By the way Mr. Buffet is not known for his extravagance unlike many of his Wall Street employees who are conspicuous in their display of their wealth. Mr Buffett has lived in the same house for 26 years and drives a 10-year-old Cadillac.

Other benefits from a US listing are:

- it enables takeovers to be financed in the US
- it incentivises US employees.

The drawback is that there are additional reporting requirements and compliance issues which take up valuable management time. Principally, the need for complete quarterly reporting causes significant extra work.

DEBT

The lending of cash to companies to fund their activities has been growing dramatically during the 1980s as financial markets have developed and international trade has grown. It has also been a customer-driven one, where a whole range of highly individually tailored new products has been created to satisfy the precise and often conflicting needs of companies. In particular, the growth of financial derivatives designed to reduce apparent risks to companies has been spectacular.

Debt: the reasons for borrowing
- Time scale – Quicker
- Ease of arrangement – Dealing with a small number of providers
- No ownership – No impact on control of business if conditions are complied with
- Tax deductibility – Interest payments are tax deductible

Main types of debt instrument
- Corporate Bonds
- Floating rate term loans and revolving credits
- Eurobonds
- Convertibles and warrants
- Deep discount and zero coupon bonds

Corporate bonds

Large companies with a need to borrow large sums of money prefer to raise them direct from investors. There is a saving on commission costs, and a company with a good rating can often command a very 'fine' interest rate, usually fixed. An important feature allowing these issues to succeed is the existence of a secondary market allowing investors to sell their bonds. If the market is liquid investors' confidence is high and the issue will be successful. There is also a possibility of a capital gain if current market interest rates are lower than the fixed rate being paid.

Illustrations

HANSON TRUST PLC: 10 per cent bonds, redeemable in 2006, in units of British £5,000.

This corporate bond trades at around £5,800 as interest rates have fallen. The interest received is fixed at £500, so this is a yield of 8.62 per cent on an investment of £5,800. The original investor has a capital gain of £800 in return for passing over the benefit of a guaranteed annual cash inflow of £500 until 2006.

SAATCHI AND SAATCHI: 6 per cent (convertible) unsecured loan stock redeemable in 2015 can be bought for around 86 per cent of its face value, providing a yield of almost 7 per cent. This would not be as high without the 'hope' factor of conversion in 2015. Long term optimists are required for this investment.

Without the existence of a secondary market, the companies would have had to pay a higher rate to reflect the risk of holding an unmarketable investment. Rates are still higher for corporate borrowers than for money market borrowers reflecting the extra risk.

Floating rate term loans and revolving credits

Term loans can be either floating or fixed rate. In times of rising interest rates they tend to be variable as the lender aims to benefit from higher interest rates. When interest rates are expected to fall a lender hopes to secure a current fixed rate to avoid a reduced income. Term loans have the major advantage of flexibility in comparison to bonds. They can be phased both for taking up the borrowing and for repayment. A 'revolver' allows repayment and subsequent reborrowing without the need for renegotiation and documentation.

Eurobonds

A Eurobond is a bond issued in a currency other than that of the country in which it is issued. Most are bearer bonds and interest is paid annually without deduction of tax. This preserves anonymity, which appeals to wealthy investors. Interest is often handled by paying agents who pay on presentation of 'coupons' normally attached to the bond when it is issued. The appeal of Eurobonds to borrowers lies in their two main characteristics: firstly they normally have fixed rates of interest and shorter maturities than corporate bonds; secondly there is rarely any security or collateral requirement, and the only restriction on the lender is a negative pledge clause so that if other publicly issued debt is secured the eurobonds rank equally for interest and payment.

Convertibles and Warrants

Convertible bonds or loan stocks have very similar characteristics to convertible preference shares in that they give the right to exchange them into ordinary voting shares on a predetermined basis on specified future dates. The impact of this is to increase ordinary share capital and reduce the amount of debt without repaying any cash or the investor making any further cash investment. A typical convertible loan stock is the Hanson issue, in £5,000 units in bearer form, convertible into ordinary shares on 28 February each year at the rate of one ordinary share for each 129p of loan. In the meantime investors receive interest at 10 per cent per annum, a rate reflecting market conditions on the date of issue.

Warrants give the holder the right to buy ordinary shares for cash at a predetermined price. They are normally issued as a 'sweetener' (making it taste nicer) or 'kicker' ('kicking' it into play as on a football field) to ensure the success of a debt issue. Hanson has warrants issued in 1989 giving the right to shareholders to buy ordinary shares for 300p between 28 February 1990 and 30 September 1997. They trade at around 27½p each and, if the option is not taken up, will be valueless after 30 September 1997. The value is in the belief that the Hanson share price will rise beyond 300p.

Deep discount and zero coupon bonds

Deep discount bonds are debt instruments offered for sale at a discount (technically more than 15 per cent) below the redemption value. They have a fixed redemption date so the term of the loan is known at the outset. It provides key cash flow and taxation advantages for issuers. In the extreme case of zero coupon bonds no interest is payable at all, the return to the investor being the difference between the issue price and the redemption value (see Field Group case). A deep discount bond has some, usually small, annual interest payment. The company benefits from an immediate cash flow, no interim interest payments and a cash outflow several years into the future. It is perfect financing for a major capital investment, such as a research and development project, where cash flows will not be positive for some time. The bond could be refinanced using these cash flows to service the new debt.

The taxation advantage is that tax relief can be obtained by the borrower on the accrued annual interest even though it is not paid until the redemption date. This further enhances the cash flow benefit but is only suitable for a company with other activities generating a tax liability. The investor only pays tax when actual income is received.

Although there are great advantages to the borrower, it is more difficult to persuade a lender unless there are specific reasons for not wanting income until some years in the future. The risk attached to an investment now producing no income and relying on a borrower to pay a large sum 10 or 20 years from now has to be very great. This type of finance is restricted to very large, stable companies with almost total certainty of being in existence for the foreseeable future. The kind of company most likely to have these characteristics is a utility – gas, water, electricity or telecommunications. For example, BT plc has an issue of zero coupon bonds repayable in 2000.

MAKING THE FUNDING DECISION

The decision to borrow and choice of instrument are influenced by the sources available to the company and its individual needs. The sources available are related to the size of the company (see Figure 2.1) and are linked to vague economic transaction options for raising it. Funding decisions need to consider not only each individual borrowing but also the impact on the existing capital structure.

Debt – Framework for funding decisions

- Cash flows
- Fixed *v*. floating rate
- Maturity profile
- Covenants
- Currencies

FRAMEWORK FOR FUNDING

Cash flows

It is vital that the cash flow position of the company is determined and controlled to ensure that commitments to paying interest and capital can be fulfilled. Failure to meet clearly defined cash payments is the biggest single source of company failure, particularly where it involves breaches in covenants.

Fixed *v*. floating rate

The sophisticated financial instruments available today have enabled the risk to be eliminated from this decision. To put it simply, the decision is based on a view of the likely trend in interest rates over the expected life of the loan. Any analysis of interest rate forecasts and actual numbers will prove that forecasting helps half of the time but not during the other half – the problem is which half. An analysis of the causes for interest changes

SOURCES OF FINANCE RELATED TO SIZE OF COMPANY

Sources

Size	Equity	Debt
Small		
Medium } Private	Limited to individual shareholders	Limited often by personal guarantee and collateral
Large	Venture capital	Available in relatively limited quantities
PLC		
Listed	Wider public audience institutions	Practically unlimited
Internationally Listed	Even wider – countries where listed on local stock exchange	Practically unlimited
Large		

Figure 2.1

will help to explain why the job of the forecaster is a difficult one. Perhaps the most recent stark example is the departure of sterling from the Exchange Rate Mechanism (ERM) of the European Monetary System (EMS) in September 1992. Within 14 months rates had fallen from 10 per cent to 5 ½ per cent. The departure was unexpected – 'membership was a central plank of Government policy' (as both John Major and Norman Lamont (then chancellor of the exchequer) insisted repeatedly until the last moment before the departure was announced) and one of the public justifications for entry to the EMS was 'a reduction in interest rates'. Indeed, when sterling entered, in October 1990, rates fell from 11 per cent to 10 per cent.

Maturity profile

Much of corporate borrowing is never repaid, being refinanced in a different form – rolled-over or replaced by the proceeds from a rights issue. The importance of an even maturity profile is to reduce the peaks when large repayments become due. As many loans are theoretically repayable many years in the future the situation could have changed in a number of areas:

- the state of the general economic environment
- the state of specific countries and markets in which the business operates
- the key currency relationships
- the state of the specific industry
- the state of the company.

Covenants

Banks and other lenders have two principal financial criteria for making their lending decisions:

- can the business make the regular interest payments?
- can the business repay the capital sums as scheduled?

They aim to control and restrict the way the business operates to ensure these cash flows are available by the use of covenants – legal restrictions. Typical covenants are:

- **Working capital – minimum figure.** The purpose here is to ensure that sufficient cash or short term assets exist to enable the regular interest payments to be made without affecting the long term operation of the business. For example, if the interest payment was made by not paying creditors, their patience might be stretched and supplies stopped. This covenant ensures that the business has sufficient total funding for adequate working capital and manages its short term assets and liabilities efficiently.
- **Interest cover.** The purpose here is to highlight the proportion of profit paid in interest. Where this proportion is rising due to higher interest rates or lower profit it may well predict future cash flow problems.
- **Cash flow cover.** This is an alternative measure relating cash interest payments more closely to the cash flow of the business.
- **Dividend constraint.** Dividend always competes with alternative homes for cash, particularly interest payments and capex. In order to ensure interest is the first in the queue, possibly encouraging capex to follow, the level of dividend payment would be restricted, perhaps to an annual percentage increase or a limited proportion of distributable profit.
- **Negative pledge clause.** This is an agreement that no further borrowing can be undertaken without the permission of existing lenders. This protects their claim on assets.
- **Alienation of assets clause.** This further strengthens the lenders' collateral position. Permission would be needed to sell any company assets. For practical purposes a minimum value would be applied.

Currencies

Decisions on borrowing in currencies is encouraged by financial reporting systems which require the conversion of profits, losses, assets and liabilities into the domestic currency of the country where the company is registered. If all the borrowings were in sterling and international investment were in other currencies then the balance sheet would be distorted annually, assuming the most common accounting policy of converting at year-end exchange rates. A way to avoid this is to raise finance in the same currency as the asset investment.

Illustration

Gardner Merchant Services Group is Europe's largest contract caterer. It was formerly part of the Forte Group and became independent Stock Exchange following a management buyout. Flotation in summer 1994 completed a £240m financing package, including:

£155 million 5-year loan – to refinance existing borrowings

$100m (£65m) 5-year loan – to fund the acquisition of the Morrison Hospitality and Restaurant Group in the US for $100m

£20m 5-year multi-currency working capital facility – to enable short term funding in a range of European currencies or US$.

RATINGS

Background

It has been common practice in the US for many years to rely on the opinion of a professional agency in assessing the creditworthiness of a borrower. There has until the late 1980s been an effective duopoly in the rating business. The two prominent firms are Moody's (owned by Dunn & Bradstreet) and Standard and Poor's (owned by McGraw Hill). Both agencies expanded into Europe in the 1980s and a British competitor, IBCA, emerged, specialising initially in rating banks, but now developing into the corporate market.

The rating process

The rating process, which is paid for by the client company, can best be described as a forensic examination carried out whilst the patient is still alive. The rating is 'refreshed', at least half-yearly, to provide an up-to-date picture to current and prospective lenders. This process is here to stay and will require proper attention from senor finance people. The factors examined during the process are:

Industry sector

- general economic position
- competition
- cyclical influences
- impact of regulation

Company characteristics

- quality of management (the single most important criterion)
- earnings (trend *and* cost base)
- financial position (conventional ratios together with asset quality and cash flow measures)
- accounting policies

Company debt

- specific analysis of existing debt, including security covenant and legal constraints.

The rating results

Table 2.7   Comparative credit ratings

	IBCA	*Moody's*	*Standard & Poor's*
Top grades	AAA	Aaa	AAA
	AA+	Aa1	AA+
	AA–	Aa3	AA–
Investment grades	A+	A1	A+
	A	A2	A
	BBB–	Baa3	BBB–
Speculative grades	B+	Ba1	BB+
	C	C	D

Table 2.7 (which has been compressed) shows how the ratings are expressed. The lower the rating, the higher the rate of interest payable on debt. Some illustrations of ratings are:

Unilever	AAA	Standard & Poor's
SmithKline Beecham	Aa3	Moody's
Hanson	AA	IBCA
Industrial Bank of Japan	A1	Moody's

ALTERNATIVE SOURCES OF FINANCE

Leasing

An alternative source of finance for asset funding is to make an arrangement for use of the asset which does not involve ownership. The commonest form is leasing, although contract hire is also a popular form. The basic difference is that contract hire incorporates a greater service element, typically including maintenance. Hire purchase is a similar method, involving frequent regular 'hire' payments; but ownership does eventually pass to the hirer on completion of the scheduled payments. A cash deficit is normally a feature of this method.

Leasing finance provided in 1993 was more than £13.5bn, with a significant proportion given to smaller companies. Lower interest rates in the 1990s have encouraged some movement towards hire purchase, with a growth of 38 per cent in the first half of 1994 to £6bn. Leasing in contrast grew only 1 per cent to £5.2bn in the same period.

A lease can be legally defined as a contract between a lessor and a lessee for the hire of a specific asset. The lessor retains ownership of the asset but conveys the right to the use of the asset to the lessee for an agreed period of time in return for the payment of specified rentals.

Two types of leasing arrangement exist: an **operating** lease and a **finance** lease. An operating lease is one which does not substantially transfer the risks and rewards of ownership of the lessee. The lessor carries the disposal and resale risks that come with asset ownership. Under current US and UK accounting standards they are 'off balance sheet', which means that the future payments under the terms of the lease have not been accumulated and stated as a liability on the balance sheet (a process known as 'capitalising the lease'). A finance lease is one where the lessor can expect to recover the original investment plus a required rate of return from the contractual payments agreed in the lease. The risks remaining with the lessor are essentially credit risks associated with the ability of the lessee to meet the contractual payments and, to a lesser extent, the underlying value of the asset should the lease be terminated early. A finance lease has to be capitalised and treated as a liability on the balance sheet.

An operating lease can be for periods significantly shorter than the useful life of the asset, and the lessor will frequently be responsible for insurance and maintenance. However, the lessor cannot, as he can under a finance lease, accurately assess the financial return at the beginning, and to compensate for these higher risks a higher return is expected.

Leasing is a frequent component in financing some capital expenditure. It is commonly used in funding the provision of vehicles, construction plant and office machinery. There are several reasons for this:

- it reduces the initial amount of cash needed to finance the project
- it enables cash outflows to be met from cash inflows from an operational project
- there can be tax advantages. A business may not be sufficiently profitable in various phases of development to be able to utilise writing down allowances, which can be passed on by a lessor in the form of lower leasing charges
- the risk to the business is reduced. It is protected from the responsibility of servicing and maintenance and from falling values due to, for example, the environmental protection legislation or the impact of inflation
- greater flexibility in making strategic and operational investment decisions is possible as the business is not tied to the result of historic decisions, taken in a different era and environment.

There are two inter-related downsides to leasing:

- the business is unable to benefit from appreciating asset values
- as the assets are not owned they cannot be used as collateral for loans. Secured borrowings attract a lower rate of interest.

The factors to be evaluated in taking the final decision can be summarised thus:

- Is asset ownership relevant
  - to provide collateral?
  - to benefit from appreciating values?
- Is the asset likely to be needed by the business for the 'planned future'?
  - How specialist is its purpose?
  - Can it be converted to alternative use if plans are changed?
  - At what cost?
- Can the business absorb the allowances against tax for the relevant period?
- Finally, perhaps critically, is the cash available to make the purchase?
  - If borrowing is necessary what impact will this have on the rest of the business?
  - If the project is big enough to warrant equity finance how will this affect the ownership structure, dividend needs, etc?

SHORT TERM FUNDING

Short term assets – mainly inventories of all types and receivables – can be financed by long term debt or equity capital. Assuming these are scarce resources they should be used sparingly where they are vital – largely in financing the establishment and long term growth of the company. If short term funding is available it adds to the overall sources of finance to a business and should be used where it is cost-effective.

INDIVIDUAL SOURCES OF SHORT TERM FUNDING

Bank overdraft

The amount of money which can be borrowed (known as the 'facility') and the basis for calculating the interest rate chargeable (usually a number 'over base rate') are agreed in advance and are normally reviewable after six months. The merits of the arrangement are clear:

- cheapness – arrangement fee as a set-up cost only – interest calculated on a daily basis
- speed – quick to arrange

- flexibility – the facility can be used to the limit or not at all.

The down-side is one of monitoring – providing accounts, cash flow statements and generally being subject to some external control.

Delayed payables

This is surely an ideal way of funding a business – no arrangement fees, quickly put in place and interest-free. All of these are true, but care is needed in judging how far to stretch the payment date. If supplier patience is pushed to the limit this can lead to poor service, disrupted deliveries and ultimately the withdrawal of all credit facilities. The costs of any of these ultimately far exceed any savings on delayed payment.

Debt factoring

Traditionally used by small companies with less than £5m turnover this has benefits of releasing cash 'invested' in debtors. The down-side is the relatively high cost, perhaps 7 per cent over borrowing base rates. There can be considerable efforts involved in setting up special bank accounts and identifying which debts are 'factored'. A costly alternative is to hand over the entire invoicing and credit control function to the factoring company.

There is a stigma attached to a company which has resorted to using this service. It is perceived to be a higher credit risk, largely because it has had to take on higher-cost finance, implying that more conventional lower-cost sources were not available.

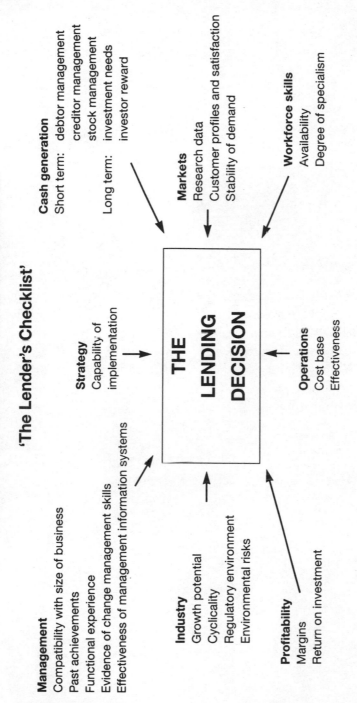

FACTORS INFLUENCING A LENDING DECISION

'The Lender's Checklist'

Management
Compatibility with size of business
Past achievements
Functional experience
Evidence of change management skills
Effectiveness of management information systems

Strategy
Capability of implementation

Industry
Growth potential
Cyclicality
Regulatory environment
Environmental risks

Profitability
Margins
Return on investment

Cash generation
Short term: debtor management
              creditor management
              stock management
Long term: investment needs
              investor reward

Markets
Research data
Customer profiles and satisfaction
Stability of demand

Workforce skills
Availability
Degree of specialism

Operations
Cost base
Effectiveness

THE
LENDING
DECISION

Figure 2.2

3

THE CAPITAL INVESTMENT DECISION

CHAPTER OBJECTIVES

- To emphasise the importance of the capital investment (capex) decision
- To describe the nature of capex
- To record the reasons for making capex
- To outline the techniques involved in capex appraisal
- To illustrate the portfolio effect of a range of capex projects
- To summarise the main stages in the capex decision-making process
- To examine the critical issues in making the capex decision:
  setting the discount rate
  evaluating and incorporating risk
  integrating non-financial factors
  allowing for the impact of inflation and deflation
- To demonstrate the effect of capital investment on shareholder value

---

'The only member of the board who must always be consulted on every strategic decision is the financial director.'

Sir John Harvey Jones, former Chairman ICI

Capital investment decisions are the most important financial decisions made in the company because they:

- involve relatively large amounts of cash
- are invariably long term

- are often either of little value if the project does not reach completion, or very costly to change.

WHAT ARE CAPITAL INVESTMENTS?

Essentially, they involve the commitment of cash now or in the near future in the hope of receiving a return in the (often distant) future (see Clarke Foods case). They have the following characteristics:

- a minimum value, determined by the board
- they appear on the balance sheet as a fixed or long term asset
- they are usually depreciated for a period of time or have their value reviewed regularly. The period of time is normally their useful life to the business but this may be an arbitrary decision
- they are purchased primarily for *use* in the business rather than for *resale*
- they are owned and controlled by the business.

Recent debate on the presentation of accounting information has raised the issue of investment in intangibles such as brands, people development, computer software, research and new product development. In the 1980s world of creative accounting, valuations of intangibles appeared on the balance sheets. Perhaps in the future, if they are to be treated as fixed assets, expenditure on them ought to be appraised using the same techniques as for the more traditional capital projects.

WHY SHOULD COMPANIES INVEST IN THE FUTURE?

- To balance capacity with demand
- To maintain or increase competitive advantage
- To maintain or increase market share
- To maintain profitability
- To exploit the benefits of new technology
- To comply with statutory requirements
- To protect existing business

- To develop new products or services.

Capital investment should be directed towards achieving the strategic objectives of the company which are focused on enhancing shareholder value.

HOW ARE CAPITAL INVESTMENT PROJECTS APPRAISED?

Individual capital projects should be appraised and their impact on the financial performance of the business evaluated. The techniques used to evaluate their viability take in three variables: cash, time and risk. There are three main evaluation techniques:

- payback period
- accounting rate of return
- discounted cash flow (DCF)
  - Net Present Value (NPV) £
  - Internal Rate of Return (IRR) per cent

Payback period

This is simply the number of years a project takes to return all the cash invested. Its key features are:

Strengths
- It is simple to calculate, showing when the cash is returned to the business for reinvestment.
- It indicates the degree of risk attached to a project. Risk increases as the payback period lengthens.

Weaknesses
- It fails to differentiate between projects returning cash very early in their life.
- It fails to show returns after the payback period.
- In its purest form it does not allow for any interest that would be gained if the money were to be invested in another way, or for the cost of capital required to fund the investment.

Table 3.1

| | Forecasted cash flows | | | |
| | Project A | | Project B | |
Year	Annual returns	Cumulative returns	Annual returns	Cumulative returns
0	−10,000	−10,000	−10,000	−10,000
1	+2,000	−8,000	+1,000	−9,000
2	+2,000	−6,000	+2,000	−7,000
3	+2,000	−4,000	+3,000	−4,000
4	+2,000	−2,000	+4,000	0
5	+2,000	0	+3,000	3,000
6			+2,000	5,000
7			+1,000	6,000
Payback period	5 years		4 years	

In Table 3.1 the payback period is shorter for Project B and it is projected to continue earning after achieving payback.

Accounting rate of return

This is the average annual profits, as a percentage of the average investment. Its key features are:

- being profit-based it equates with existing divisional and company financial reporting systems
- the timing of the cash inflows is ignored.

Illustration

Project cost   £90,000

Residual value   £10,000

Depreciation straight line over four years   (£90,000 − £10,000) ÷ 4 = £20,000

Year	Net profits (£)
1	20,000
2	30,000
3	30,000
4	25,000
5	20,000
	125,000

Average annual profits   £125,000 ÷ 5 – £20,000

(after depreciation)   = £5,000

Average investment   (£90,000 + £10,000) ÷ 2

                                        = £50,000

Accounting rate of return (£5,000 ÷ £50,000) × (100 ÷ 1) = 10 per cent

Discounted cash flows (DCF)

The discounting process is the way in which the time value of money is incorporated into an investment decision. The time value of money is simply a recognition of the fact that £1 today is of greater value than £1 in the future because money carries with it an ability to earn interest. Present value tables (see Table 3.2) are used to bring sums of money which will be received in the future back to their value today.

Table 3.2   Present Value of £1

Years hence	1%	2%	4%	6%	8%	10%	12%	14%	15%
1	0.990	0.980	0.962	0.943	0.926	0.909	0.893	0.877	0.870
2	0.980	0.961	0.925	0.890	0.857	0.826	0.797	0.769	0.756
3	0.971	0.942	0.889	0.840	0.794	0.751	0.712	0.675	0.658
4	0.961	0.924	0.855	0.792	0.735	0.683	0.636	0.592	0.572
5	0.951	0.906	0.822	0.747	0.681	0.621	0.567	0.519	0.497
6	0.942	0.888	0.790	0.705	0.630	0.564	0.507	0.456	0.432
7	0.933	0.871	0.760	0.665	0.583	0.513	0.452	0.400	0.376
8	0.923	0.853	0.731	0.627	0.540	0.467	0.404	0.351	0.327
9	0.914	0.837	0.703	0.592	0.500	0.424	0.361	0.308	0.284
10	0.905	0.820	0.676	0.558	0.463	0.386	0.322	0.270	0.247
11	0.896	0.804	0.650	0.527	0.429	0.350	0.287	0.237	0.215
12	0.887	0.788	0.625	0.497	0.397	0.319	0.257	0.208	0.187
13	0.879	0.773	0.601	0.469	0.368	0.290	0.229	0.182	0.163
14	0.870	0.758	0.577	0.442	0.340	0.263	0.205	0.160	0.141
15	0.861	0.743	0.555	0.417	0.315	0.239	0.183	0.140	0.123
16	0.853	0.728	0.534	0.394	0.292	0.218	0.163	0.123	0.107
17	0.844	0.714	0.513	0.371	0.270	0.198	0.146	0.108	0.093
18	0.836	0.700	0.494	0.350	0.250	0.180	0.130	0.095	0.081
19	0.828	0.686	0.475	0.331	0.232	0.164	0.116	0.083	0.070
20	0.820	0.673	0.456	0.312	0.215	0.149	0.104	0.073	0.061

£1 received in seven years' time with an interest rate of 14 per cent is worth 40p today.

Time value is not the same thing as changes in purchasing power, which are affected by inflation or deflation in the price of goods or services.

Illustration

If a project were to produce a return in cash of £100,000 in nine years' time and the initial cash investment of £50,000 was borrowed today at a fixed rate of 8 per cent, the project would exactly break even or 'wash its face'*. In other words, the value today of £100,000 to be received in five years' time is £50,000. There are two ways of expressing the output from the discounting process:

- the **Net Present Value (NPV)** is the cash surplus produced from the project expressed in present day values
- the **Internal Rate of Return (IRR)** is the rate of return achieved by the project from the cash invested. It assumes that any surplus cash is available to be reinvested in other projects. The IRR is the discount rate which gives a project a net present value of zero.

*An American expression meaning 'come out looking clean' or unchanged i.e. without a loss, but maybe very little profit.

Illustration

A project has the following forecast cash flows:

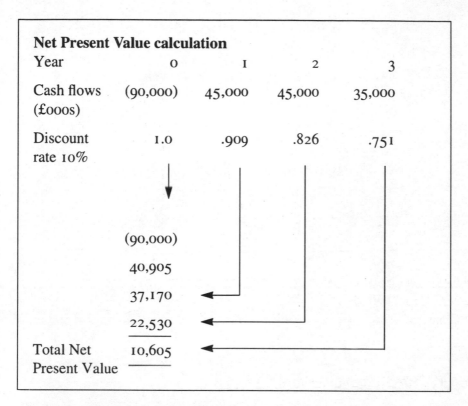

Net Present Value calculation

Year	0	1	2	3
Cash flows (£000s)	(90,000)	45,000	45,000	35,000
Discount rate 10%	1.0	.909	.826	.751

	(90,000)
	40,905
	37,170
	22,530
Total Net Present Value	10,605

The NPV is positive, which means:

- the IRR of the project is greater than the discount rate
- if cash had to be borrowed at 10 per cent per annum the cash flows from the project would enable interest and capital to be repaid in three years and leave a surplus of £10,605 in present value terms.

Although the rate of return exceeds 10 per cent, does it exceed 20 per cent?

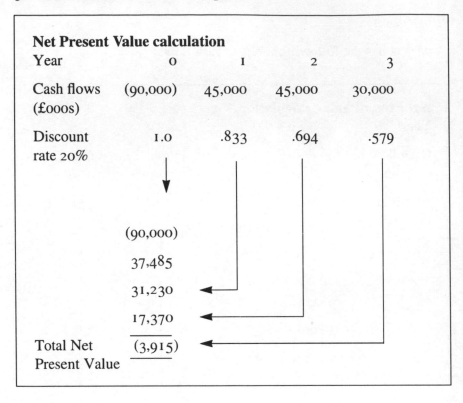

Net Present Value calculation

Year	0	1	2	3
Cash flows (£000s)	(90,000)	45,000	45,000	30,000
Discount rate 20%	1.0	.833	.694	·579

(90,000)

37,485

31,230

17,370

Total Net Present Value   (3,915)

The NPV is negative, which means:

- the IRR of the project is less than the discount rate
- if cash had to be borrowed at 20 per cent per annum the cash flows from the project would give a shortfall of £3,915 in present value terms.

The calculation of the actual IRR is completed by interpolation:

Base discount rate	10%	NPV	£10,605
Higher discount rate	20%	NPV	(£3,915)
Interval between discount rate	10%		
Range of Net Present Values			£14,520

The aim is to find the rate of return. This will be the discount rate which produces a NPV of zero.

20%	?%	10%
I ———————————————————— I
(3,915)	0	10,605

The interpolation formula is:

$$10\% + \frac{(10,605}{(14,520} \quad \frac{10)}{100)}$$

$$= 10\% + 7\% = 17\%$$

As a further check and proof:

	Capital outstanding (£)	Add interest at 17% (£)	Total debt at year end (£)	Less repayments from cash flow (£)	Closing end of year figure (£)
YEAR 1	90,000	15,300	105,300	(45,000)	60,300
YEAR 2	60,300	10,300	70,600	(45,000)	25,600
YEAR 3	25,600	4,400	30,000	(30,000)	–

Benefits of the IRR

● It may be taken as the highest rate the company can borrow to finance this project.
● It can be used to compare investments

THE PORTFOLIO EFFECT

The attitude to risk is often a strategic decision at board level. Given the relationship between risk and return, the way in which a business can increase its return is by taking a higher level of risk. This can be achieved either by moving the investment portfolio as a whole along the risk axis or making individual investments in higher risk areas (see Figure 3.1).

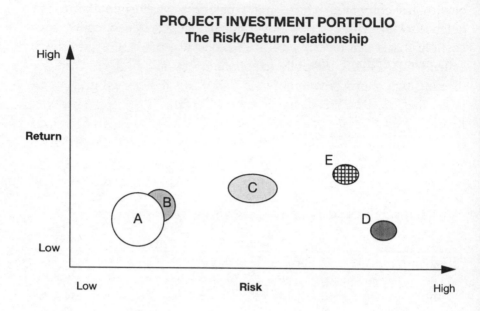

Figure 3.1

The concept is presented diagrammatically in Figure 3.1 taking as an illustration the project portfolio of a UK-based mainly food retailing group.

A   is the main domestic core business producing a relatively low return, but the risk is correspondingly low.

B   is incorporating a bigger proportion of non-food products. The return is higher, but the risk may not be fully compensated for.

C   is a major investment in a retailing business in the US. The risk has increased but the return has not.

D   is a pilot operation in St Petersburg. It is a single unit which in this case will never produce a satisfactory return on its own but may produce excellent market research data for the evaluation of future investment.

E   is a joint venture with a retailer of complementary products on the same site.

A successful example of a D type project would be RACAL, a UK electronics company, whose main business was originally in the defence sector, with low risk Government contracts issued mainly on a cost plus basis. An investment of £250,000 was made in a subsidiary called VODAFONE, a mobile telephone operator, a high risk venture offering high returns. Eventually the VODAFONE business grew to be larger than the RACAL business and the VODAFONE company was floated separately on the London Stock Exchange. In summer 1994 RACAL had a market capitalisation of £629.5m, while VODAFONE was nearly nine times larger at £5,282m.

THE CAPEX DECISION-MAKING PROCESS

The first stage is to accurately and fully describe the projects. Often the decision-making is remote from the origin of the investment proposal. Normally, small projects can be approved locally, where there is detailed knowledge of the need. The very largest projects require main board approval, and the proposal should clearly and persuasively describe the project.

All major projects would usually need to be sponsored by a member of the main board. It is necessary that the sponsor be committed and fully supportive to secure approval from his colleagues. There is a legend that in one very well known FTSE Top-100 company all major capex decisions are ultimately made by the autocratic chief executive. All the usual analyses of payback DCF IRR are carried out. The proposals contain comprehensive market research data and are carefully evaluated by corporate strategists. What numbers are critical to the decision? All of the aforementioned are of course taken into account, but the critical influence is not a number, it is a signature – of the sponsoring executive. His past record in managing investments linked with his commitment to the current proposal is viewed as being the most likely indicator of success, by combining proven ability with current market and operational knowledge. There is one significant side-effect. The executives only sponsor projects that are virtually certain to achieve at least the rate of return predicted, as their reputations and the prospects for the next capex project are always dependent on the performance of the last one. The result is that projects and developments within this business tend to be low risk, where returns are more safely predictable.

The project description is the critical stage in selling the project to the business. Many good projects fail to gain acceptance because their strengths are understated at the outset. It is equally unwise to overstate the benefits from the project. The uses of a tough post-completion audit are becoming more widespread. This involves an analysis of the performance of the project, usually two years after implementation. The comparison with plans and forecasts is designed to help refine the process for preparing future proposals.

CRITICAL ISSUES

Setting the discount rate

The rate of return required from a project is influenced by a number of factors:

- the overall cost of capital in the business from all sources
- the specific cost for a project where this can be identified
- the current return achieved by the business
- the degree of risk that can be attributed to this specific project.

The setting of a discount rate is a critical management decision. If high rates are set it is difficult to find suitable projects, particularly when a risk premium has been added. The UK General Electric Company (GEC) has often been criticised in the financial press for retaining cash in the business – regularly in the £1.5bn–£2bn range – rather than invest in capital projects. In the past the company has earned considerable risk-free interest income. As rates have fallen in the 1990s the company has invested, although the major projects have been in joint ventures – GEC-Alsthom GPT (with Plessey) and with Siemens – where the risk is shared. The possibility has been raised that the rates of return demanded to compensate for additional business risk are too high. Setting too low a rate could have the effect of diluting the existing return achieved by the business.

It seems invalid to accept projects that do not meet the existing return being achieved by the business. Logically any new project must increase the risk to the business simply because it is new and additional – even by a very small amount – and this risk should be compensated for by applying a risk-adjusted rate of return.

Evaluating and incorporating risk

Academic theory and common sense thankfully coincide in supporting the view that there is a clear relationship between the amount of return likely to be produced by an investment and its level of risk. Many companies attempt to classify projects by level of risk and incorporate this into the expected rate of return (see Table 3.3).

Table 3.3

Level of risk	Typical business project	
Low	• scale expansion	{ same product and same market
	• strong associated product, e.g. beer and lager, cars and off-road vehicles • similar customer base • expertise in existing technology	
Medium	• scale expansion	{ new product or new market
	• different distribution channel • different customer base • proven technology, but no expertise or experience within the business	
High	• R&D project • reliance on unproven technology	{ new product and new market

The final step in calculating a risk-adjusted rate of return is to decide a premium to add to the existing return on capital employed within the business to reflect the additional business risk. More sophisticated versions have been developed, based on a points system which is converted to risk premia percentages. This involves producing a checklist of risk factors and attaching a number of points to each – the greater the risk, the higher the number of points.

Checklist of risk factors

- Market forecasts
  - existing
  - new
- Technology
- Competitive products
- Impact on existing business
- Core skills and competencies within the business
- Financing risks
  - debt
  - equity
- Impact of legislation
- Country risk
- Political risk
- Environmental risk

No single forecast would be an acceptable basis for making a decision. Three level PRO forecasts – Pessimistic, Realistic and Optimistic – are a minimum, combined with many interactions of sensitivity (what if?) analysis applied and the results plotted to suggest a target range.

Integrating non-financial factors into the decision-making process

It is unavoidable that some investment projects do not earn the same rate of return as the existing business. Routine replacement is often difficult to justify other than as profit 'protection'. Sample justifications in a non-financial context are:

Reasons	*Typical projects*
Corporate image	Design of company logo
	Refurbishment of reception area
Competitive action	Establishing a marketing organisation in a new region
Health, safety or environment	Internal medical facility
	Pollution control equipment
Strategic	Long term planning for replacement of existing product range

The impact of inflation and deflation

It has become easy in the 1990s to ignore inflation – in many Western economies the rate has been consistently less than 3 per cent. At these levels the impact is small, but for long term investment it is important to measure the return in real, rather than nominal, terms. Low inflation has made it difficult to increase prices and some cost increases are unavoidable in specific situations. The practice of 'gap management' – where the main relevant figure is the 'gap' or difference between cost and sales price – has developed. Where the price cannot be increased, any cost increase has had to be met by identifying a compensating saving, leaving the 'gap' protected.

The discounting process reflects only the cost of borrowing (or of lost interest if the source was an interest-bearing deposit); it does not in any way adjust for inflation and deflation.

THE IMPACT OF CAPITAL INVESTMENT ON SHAREHOLDER VALUE

The main objective of business is to maximise the wealth of the owners. In a company the owners are shareholders and their wealth can be increased in two ways:

- short term – by receiving cash or share dividends
- long term – by appreciation in the capital value of their investment.

Figure 3.2 illustrates how capital investment affects shareholders'
returns by adding value to the business.

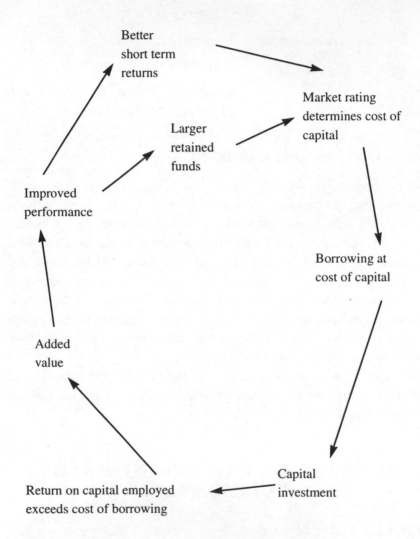

Figure 3.2

TERMS USED IN CAPITAL EXPENDITURE EVALUATION

Term	*Definition*
Capital expenditure	Expenditure on assets which will remain in the business for more than one year
Cash inflow	Money generated as income
Cash outflow	Money spent
Depreciation	The process of allocating the cost of an asset over the predicted years of its useful life in the business
DCF return	The discounted cash flow return, which is adjusted for the time value of money
Net Present Value	The total of all cash inflows and cash outflows, adjusting for the time value of money to bring them to a present-day equivalent
Payback period	The number of years taken for the cash inflows to equal the cash outflows
Present value of £1	The value today of £1 receivable at some time in the future
Residual value	The value of a project at the end of an investment period

4

MANAGING THE FINANCES OF BUSINESS DEVELOPMENT

CHAPTER OBJECTIVES
- **To examine the reasons for developing the business**
- **To discuss the strategies for developing the business**
- **To introduce the financial implications of business development**

Expansion is an important objective for many businesses. The financial implication of growth is a continuing need for cash for both long and short term funding. Managing the cash flow properly will reduce the need for shareholders and lenders to finance long term growth, and firm control of working capital should ensure short term needs are minimised. Effective financial management of business growth needs to incorporate both elements.

REASONS FOR DEVELOPING THE BUSINESS

- **To ensure better asset utilisation.** Many management decisions can be justified financially by covering fixed costs over a greater volume of output. It has been a reluctant policy for some companies in the recession-hit era of the late 1980s and early 1990s to accept volume orders at reduced margins simply to raise utilisation of assets. Only if surplus capacity exists can this be a positive decision and then only if a worthwhile contribution can be made. Installing surplus capacity to fill with marginally profitable orders does not make sense at all in the long term and only rarely in the short term.

- **To obtain additional or special skills.** A sensible motive to ensure that the range of products and services offered by the business is expanded, updated and differentiated, allowing market share and customer loyalty to be retained.
- **To secure supplies and maintain quality.** A valid reason in support of the remainder of business as it contributes to maintaining the current profitability. This reason can be very important, for example where very high specification components are needed.
- **To enhance earnings per share.** A common reason historically relating to when earnings per share was a key performance indicator. It used to work like this. The company with a high price-earnings (P/E) ratio buys a company with a low P/E. Because of its high share price relatively few shares need to be issued to make the acquisition. The market then values the *combined* company at the higher P/E. Clearly everybody wins – in the short term. After that the acquired company has to perform as well as the acquiror – not easy, which is probably why it was a takeover target in the first place.
- **To utilise borrowing capacity.** Again, a popular reason in the past. A high level of gearing has been viewed conventionally as an additional risk factor, and higher interest rates are often charged. The logic was that unused collateral available would lower the rate, thus providing a tangible financial cost saving. The enormous range of competitive sources of finances has reduced the importance of this as a pure motive. Of greater benefit is the possibility of role and leaseback, giving a valuable immediate cash injection to the business.

STRATEGIES FOR DEVELOPING THE BUSINESS

Expansion can be achieved by a number of strategies:

- organic business development
- strategic alliances/joint ventures
- minority equity stake
- majority equity stake
- merger
- outright acquisition.

Table 4.1   Growth strategies summary

	Pace	Risk and financial commitment	Control	Accounting policy
Organic	Slow	Low	Total	Unaffected
Strategic alliance/joint venture	Fast	Low	Partial	Associate
Minority equity stake	Fast	Low	Minority	Associate
Majority equity stake	Normally fast	High	Majority	Subsidiary
Acquisition	Normally fast	High	Majority	Acquisition or merger accounting

Table 4.2   Strategy selection

Reason for growth	Appropriate strategy
To ensure better asset utilisation	All
To obtain additional or special skills	All
To secure supplies and maintain quality	All
To enhance earnings per share	Outright acquisition to get full benefit
To utilise borrowing capacity	Outright acquisition to get full benefit
To generate cash	Outright acquisition

Organic business development

- **Slow pace.** The speed of growth is limited by the existing resources of the business, which can only be gradually increased if effective management and control are to be maintained. The major UK supermarket groups, Tesco and Sainsbury's, are excellent examples of huge organic growth in recent years. Only in rare cases have they used acquisition. In summer 1994 they competed with each other for a small Scottish group, William Low. Tesco won but had to pay 60 per cent more than its original bid.
- **Risk and financial commitment.** The slow, more cautious approach will reduce the overall risk by ensuring a greater and deeper knowledge of the way the industry, the business and its suppliers work together to meet the needs of the customer. More controlled gradual investment will reduce the financial risk.

Strategic alliance/joint venture

- **Fast pace.** In some ways this method can be even more rapid than acquisition as there will be no hostility, fewer legal formalities and greater co-operation. The problems of post-acquisition management and organisation are greatly reduced. The ideal operation combines local market knowledge or specific technology experience with an existing product or concept.
- **Risk and financial commitment**. These are much reduced by the combination of skills and knowledge brought to the business. The sharing of investment reduces the commitment but limits the shared return from the business. An example of this is GEC, the UK electronic, engineering and defence contractor, which has a wide variety of joint ventures with Alsthom of France, Siemens of Germany and Plessey in the UK. Many major future developments in the telecommunications and media industry will be in this form.
- **Political, regulatory and cultural.** In areas of the world such as the Gulf, parts of Asia Pacific and Eastern Europe it is either impractical or even impossible to develop a business without a local partner.

Minority equity stake

- **Fast pace.** The existing management normally continues, and influence, but not control, is attained. Without control there is a risk, but it may be the only way the opportunity can be taken forward.
- **Risk and financial commitment.** Often both the amount of cash committed and the risk are low. The return from this type of investment is frequently improved by enhanced returns from other parts of the business. This type of arrangement is particularly suitable, for example, in distribution and local marketing where the main business is manufacturing.

Majority equity stake

- **Fast pace.** Normally there is a willing seller and a high degree of management participation. This enables rapid and usually relatively easy co-operation. Typically, the business will maintain a strong, separate identity.
- **Risk and financial commitment.** Owning the majority of a business has dual impact on the risk – less from the control point of view but greater as the cash investment rises. It will affect the reported financial results and must also be consolidated with the financial numbers for the rest of the business, treating the proportion not owned as a minority interest.

Merger

- **Relatively fast pace.** A merger is the combination of two (or more) companies into one. The implication is that it is friendly and handled in more of a sensitive way than an acquisition. The same benefits – market share, capacity, product range, turnover and assets – will still be apparent, but they are shared rather than acquired and are likely to take longer to come through.
- **Risk and financial commitment.** Similar to outright acquisition, particularly if it is for 'paper', when shareholders of the acquired company would become shareholders in the combined enterprise. In practice few true mergers really exist; there is usually a stronger partner in terms of size, assets, profitability or cash generation. The

composition of the new board and holders of the key functions usually indicate where the power lies.

Outright acquisition

- **Fast pace.** Initially the acquisition of the entire business must be viewed as being a fast alternative. Once complete ownership is established changes can, in theory, be rapidly executed. In practice it rarely proves that simple, and numerous acquisitions have failed in this phase. Many others just take much more time to integrate and deliver tangible financial benefits than was envisaged at the outset.
- **Risk and financial commitment.** Acquisition is often the biggest capital expenditure decision made by a business. Generally it increases the risk, particularly if the acquisition is unrelated to the existing activities of the main business. Total ownership does mean that all the rewards go to the acquiror. Consolidation with the financial numbers for the rest of the business is required and now has to be separately identified in the year of acquisition, thus highlighting immediately the early impact. Strategies are influenced by the reason for growth; acquisition is not the only route and is often the most costly, with the highest risk.

The selection of which of the above is appropriate should be made in each specific situation, considering factors such as:
- required pace of development
- need for control
- accounting issues
- legal issues
- tax issues
- regulatory controls
- local customs and culture
- potential investment incentives
- environmental aspects
- economic forecasts

And finally, most important of all is **availability** – particularly for total or partial acquisition of an existing business.

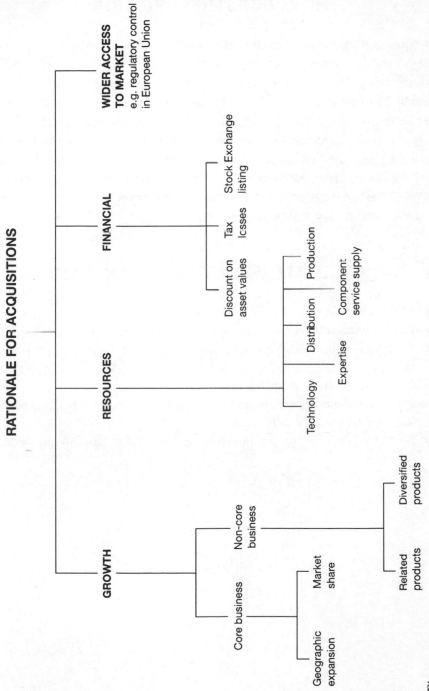

RATIONALE FOR ACQUISITIONS

GROWTH

Core business

Geographic expansion

Market share

Non-core business

Related products

Diversified products

RESOURCES

Technology

Expertise

Distribution

Production

Component service supply

FINANCIAL

Discount on asset values

Tax losses

Stock Exchange listing

WIDER ACCESS TO MARKET
e.g. regulatory control in European Union

Figure 4.1

THE ACQUISITION DECISION

Acquisitions are usually the largest capital investments made by a business. The big sums of money involved are only the first part of the story. Integration, restructuring and rationalisation expenses are as much part of the overall cost of the acquisition as the original price, even though they are incurred in the post-acquisition phase. The biggest loss can come later if the acquisition performance is disappointing and the divestment route is taken. Figure 4.1 shows how it should not be done, but there is an element of truth in it for some companies that were caught up in the 'acquisition fever' of the mid-to-late 1980s – and it may still be happening.

HOW TO MAKE AN ACQUISITION FAIL

- Make a hostile bid.
- Pay a premium to win.
- Set a high return on investment target, reflecting the high acquisition cost.
- Fail to meet an over-ambitious target.
- Cut costs and reduce short and long term investment in the business.
- Watch performance deteriorate.
- Sell at a discount to the purchase price – 'not part of our "core business" '.

5

COMPANY VALUATION

CHAPTER OBJECTIVES
- **To describe the methods of valuing a business**
- **To compare and contrast the different methods**
- **To help to identify the right price**
- **To outline the methods of financing the acquisition of a business**
- **To produce a checklist of information helpful to the valuation process**

The valuation of a business is important for the purposes of:

- acquisition
- divestment
- management buy-out
- management buy-in
- measurement of corporate performance.

If the company has its shares traded on a public stock market a base value is already established. Typically, an acquiror will have to pay 30 per cent above current market capitalisation to persuade share-holders to sell. It is important that this premium above market value is justified by determining the value to the acquiror of the specific benefits of the acquisition. Valuation methods can be based around three criteria:

- asset
- market
- cash flow.

An important aspect of valuation is to realise that it is the future you are buying but you have to *pay for the past*.

ASSET BASED

Part of the value of a business is the worth of the assets acquired. They can be valued in a number of ways:

- balance sheet value
- market value
- replacement value
- value to the existing business
- value to the acquiror.

Balance sheet value

The value of an asset in the balance sheet is historic cost less accumulated depreciation as determined by the accounting policy and approved by the auditors. It will be a coincidence if this value represents either its real value to the business or its external market value. It is useful only in providing an indication of what the assets are worth to the business and, in some cases, particularly regarding debtors, a close idea of the likely realisation amount if they are converted to cash individually.

Replacement cost is another alternative cost-based method, but the possibility of re-creating a unique entity is almost inconceivable to plan, let alone value. In reality, unless the business needs these specific assets their value is the amount they can be sold for or the cost of an equivalent asset.

Non-balance sheet assets

Many assets of significant value do not appear in the balance sheet. There are three principal reasons for this:

- accounting standards and policies
- complexity of valuation
- difficulties in establishing ownership and degree of control.

Most of the assets in this group come under the heading of **intangibles**. Common examples are: brands, people, management information systems, distribution agreements, technical expertise, intellectual property, customer list and future order position. These assets are likely to represent the major reason for the acquisition and the largest part of the value.

Valuing the intangibles

The wave of acquisitions and mergers in the 1980s generated a need to justify the ever-increasing prices paid for businesses. The important aspect of this was the recognition that substantial amounts of money were being paid for the intangible elements of a business. Two significant changes in the international financial environment have changed the way tangible assets are financed and valued:

- **Inflation levels.** The almost world-wide reduction in levels of inflation during the 1990s has limited the potential appreciation in tangible asset values such as property (real estate) and stocks (inventory). Most commodity prices have been depressed, due mainly to the impact of the recessionary trading conditions of the late 1980s and early 1990s.
- **Asset financing and ownership.** Fewer assets are now purchased by businesses as they aim to reduce the permanent investment by paying for use rather than taking on the obligations of ownership. These assets are mainly property and all types of machinery, equipment and vehicles. Rapidly changing technology, customer needs and potential future environmental impact costs, combined with reduced inflation levels, have made ownership less attractive. Only where the cost of hiring or leasing exceeds the financing cost of buying should buying be considered, and then only when asset appreciation or an additional reward for control, such as protecting profit, can be incorporated.

The result of these changes has increased both the importance of intangibles as unique, differentiating factors and their value as profit generators.

The need to get these assets incorporated on the balance sheet has generated research and activity in the valuation of intangibles. The focus of this work has been on brands. A specialist consultancy, Inter-brand, is active in the area and the model it has developed is gaining credibility. Current (1994) brand values produced in the US using the Interbrand formula have identified Coca-Cola as the most valuable brand, with a worth of £24bn. Other major values are:

Brand	Value	Product
Marlboro	£22bn	cigarettes
Nescafé	£8bn	coffee
Kodak	£7bn	films and cameras
Microsoft	£6.5bn	computer software
Compaq	£2.7bn	computer hardware
Green Giant	£0.3bn	tinned sweetcorn

In total, the values of 290 brands were calculated. Bottom of the list was IBM, which was in the group described as having a 'negative net worth', in other words 'a competing generic product could have generated higher profits on the same level of sales'.

These values are untested in the market but there have been brand sales in recent years. An example was the repurchase in September 1994 of the brand Aspirin by the German company Bayer for £650m. It had been American-owned since 1918, having been confiscated as part of the reparations following the First World War.

Valuation bases

There are two primary bases for valuing intangible assets:

- cost based
- value based.

Cost based

Currently the way most intangible assets appear on the balance sheet is using a cost based valuation. The accountancy and auditing profession still takes comfort from being able to document a 'real money' record of an event. This is easily applicable for acquired brands and provides a basis for capitalising brand development costs. There is no support-able link that cost always translates into value, but for acquired brands there is a logic that it was bought in the open market.

As only acquired brands can be included in the balance sheet under UK accounting standards, the historic cost of brand building has been written off as an expense in the profit statement. If a home-grown brand has the ability to enable premium pricing and generate more cash than a generic product it must have a value. The Guinness stout brand, for example, cannot be shown in the balance sheet but it has a unique and enduring value.

Value based

This is primarily a cash flow driven basis. Cash, or close cash equi-valent such as shares (paper), is used to purchase an asset. Funda-mentally, its value is made up of two components: its ability to generate cash in the short term to enable the investor to be rewarded, and its ability to provide cash in the long term when it is converted into cash. The first, being nearer to today, is more certain, the second is highly volatile. The value of a brand in cash flow terms lies in its ability to generate cash in excess of an unbranded generic competitor product.

Illustration – a first stab at brand valuation

A can of a branded soft drink retails at 40p. Its generic equivalent sells at 30p. The price premium is 10p. The manufacturing costs could be identical, as the proportion of manufacturing cost to sales value in the food and drink industry is low and a branded drinks company is likely to have the expertise – and the money – to create a very efficient pro-duction facility.

If the sales volume in a market is 12 million cans per annum, then the brand premium is £1.2m (i.e. 12 million cans at 10p each). If the pro-duct has a directly attributable advertising and promotion cost of £200,000 which is sufficient to maintain the sales at that level, the net cash generation would be £1m a year.

If this earnings figure is capitalised using 5 per cent as an appropriate rate, a brand valuation of £20m results. The capitalisation process uses the same principles as the discounting process. Essentially it asks the question: if we have an investment that will produce a return of £1m per year and we could invest cash and get 5 per cent per annum interest as an alternative, what would we pay for this investment?

The answer is £20m, because £20m invested at 5 per cent per annum would produce an annual return of £1m.

It has been assumed that both investments would produce that rate of return for the foreseeable future – jargonised as 'in perpetuity'. Many brand valuation policy statements in annual reports – as in the Guinness policy quoted later – make this assumption.

MARKET BASED

The incorporation of a market discipline into a company valuation provides a valuable alternative view. If the target is a listed (quoted) company it will already have a market value (capitalisation). Although that is the value placed on it by the market, it is not the price that will persuade the shareholder to sell. Typically, a premium of 30 per cent has to be paid to ensure a successful bid. This figure may need to be increased dramatically if the bid is hostile or is contested and becomes like an auction.

An illustration of this occurred in July 1994 in the UK when bids were made for the Scottish supermarket group, William Low. The original offer of £154m was made by Tesco, which also acknowledged publicly that the real cost was £35m higher to pay for rebranding stores and integrating the computer systems. The bid was accepted by the William Low board who then recommended it to shareholders. At 56p ahead of the pre-bid market price, with profits on the slide and an admitted inability to extract any more purchase efficiencies from suppliers given the company's current size, it looked like a 'done deal'. Along came Sainsbury's the following week with an offer of £210m, to which Tesco retaliated with £247m – an increase of £93m (60 per cent) on their first offer. The Sainsbury's response was to withdraw, issuing the following statement: 'We know the value of the business and were not prepared to pay a penny more. If a rival has been forced to pay more for it, that's no bad thing.'

At least the board had a consolation prize in the end. The Chairman had share options at 227p per share, just 2p more than the 225p initial Tesco bid, leaving them worthless. The final 360p bid brought him £184,000. Other directors share £925,000 – courtesy of Sainsbury's.

Private and unlisted companies

If the target is not a publicly quoted company there is no current market price and possibly there may never have been a valuation. The technique of applying the valuation of a quoted company to an unquoted company is achieved by using the price earnings ratio (P/E). The stages involved are:

- Identify a similar quoted company to the target company being valued. 'Similar' means the company should be:
  - in the same industry sector
  - as close a competitor as possible
  - as similar in turnover as possible
  - similar in asset values. (This is not essential as the assets can be valued separately as independent from the business and incorporated in the valuation at a later stage.)
  - similar in product range.
- Take the P/E of the similar company,

  i.e. $\dfrac{\text{current market share price}}{\text{earnings per share after tax}}$

If it is difficult to find the ideal similar company take the nearest two or three and average the P/E. If problems still exist take the overall business sector P/E.

- Adjust the unquoted company's earnings as far as possible to make it comparable as a stand-alone business. This involves adding back such items as:
  - apparently excessive salaries and expenses, sometimes paid to family members more as a reward for ownership than a necessary business cost
  - potential under-declaration of profit. It is common to be conservative in accounting policies if this results in a lower tax charge and there are no anxious lenders demanding high levels of performance to ensure their support is maintained. It is not uncommon to see profits in companies like this rise for a couple of years before sale or possible flotation is planned.

Both of these and any other adjustments could need to be done in the opposite direction. The ultimate aim is to provide an earnings figure which the business is capable of producing in a typical year, after deducting costs which would be necessary to operate a business of that size.

- Apply the market company P/E ratio multiple to the profits of the unquoted company, simulating a market capitalisation value.

Illustration

A potential acquisition has been targeted by a group, the main business of which is food retailing, although it does have interests in food manufacturing and processing. Its P/E is 15, which is around the average for the sector. The potential acquisition is a private company involved in processing 'recipe dishes' with fish as the main ingredient. Recipe dishes are part-prepared meals suitable mainly for microwave cooking. The profile of the business is:

- turnover   £15m
- profit   £1.5m
- net total assets   £5m
- directors' salaries   £1m
- dividends   £500,000.

Stage 1

- **Find a similar quoted company.** As there is no specialist fish processing sector, the nearest one is food manufacturing and three companies exist with similar characteristics.

Stage 2

- **Use the quoted P/E ratio.**
  Competitor A is larger and more diverse   P/E 11.1
  Competitor B is small and very specialist   P/E 14.5
  Competitor C is small and similar but uses turkey   .
  and chicken to prepare similar products   P/E 14.1
  From the above selection it would appear that 14 is a realistic figure.

The lower P/E could be reflective of the lower popularity, arising from the higher risk attached to a more diverse company.

Stage 3

- **Adjust the unquoted company's earnings.** Using the comparable dividend yield for the quoted companies it appears that excess dividend is being paid. Add back £100,000

The directors' salaries to run a business of this size could be substantially less, even allowing for a group management charge. Add back £400,000

Total add back £500,000

Revised profit figure: existing £1.5m

add back £0.5m

£2m

With a comparable P/E of 14, the company is valued at 14 X £2m = £28m.

CASH FLOW BASED

This method relies upon the use of the discounted cash flow (DCF) technique and essentially treats the acquisition as a cash investment which will produce a pattern of cash returns in the future. A key element is the estimation of what the sale (market) value of the business will be on a selected future date – possibly a target date for sale or flotation or a pre-determined date influenced by the time horizon of the business. The process is exactly the DCF method, involving forecasts of:

- revenues from customers
- other special income
- regular costs
- on-going capex necessary to maintain the income stream
- business development costs quantified in a growing final value.

All figures are **cash**, need to be predicted accurately for **time** and subjected to sensitivity analysis to assess the most likely scenario. The selection of an appropriate discount rate is important, taking account of the factors involved in assessing the risk.

ADDITIONAL FACTORS INFLUENCING VALUATION

Other criteria which will influence the value include:

- timing
- synergy with existing businesses
- risk assessment
- strategic implications
- accounting treatment and taxation effects.

Timing

A key reason for acquisition is the time saving that will result from gaining instant access to the benefits of an operating unit. Some of these will be business-oriented and others will arise out of the accounting and taxation treatment. The alternative of organic growth is inevitably slower and could arguably carry more risk as new lessons have to be learned. Against that the costs and risk in integrated acquisitions can be enormous.

Synergy with existing businesses

Synergy was perhaps one of the most cynically over-used words of the 1980s, often used to make claims which could not be justified later. The theory is that benefits could arise from a merger. Many can be quantified and therefore form part of the financial justification for an acquisition, for example as a result of the combination of businesses from such things as a shared, integrated management information system, distribution economies and pooling of research and development funding and expertise. The practice can be that savings are decimated by the costs of co-ordination and attempting to manage a diversified business. There is also a great problem in changing the 'us versus them' syndrome. The main way companies cope with this situation is to take a soft and slow approach. The effect of this delay can be seen financially in failing to achieve the promised savings – making a return on acquisition investment even more difficult to achieve.

Risk assessment

In order to arrive at a valuation of a company, an assessment of the risk factors and an attempt to incorporate them into a target rate of return must be made. Factors determining risk in company acquisition include:

- knowledge of the business – core or diversification
- market forecasts
- competitive position
- barriers to entry
- market share
- technological expertise
- regulatory environment
- essentialness of the product.

Strategic implications

If 'synergy' ranks as one the most over-used words of the 1980s then 'strategy' has to be another. If an acquisition cannot be justified on straightforward return on investment grounds, merely describing it as 'strategic' will not help. The acquisition has to be capable of generating cash in excess of funding costs and must bring the promise of real growth in the future.

Accounting treatment and taxation effects

The vigorous growth in economic activity in the 1980s resulted in a huge increase in the volume of acquisition and merger activity. Partly as a result of this boom insufficient attention was given to maintaining and improving standards of financial reporting. The result was that some acquisitons were made without the underlying business logic, simply because they allowed earnings to be enhanced and balance sheets to be apparently stronger. Changes in the rules for financial reporting are progressively being introduced in the UK, which will severely restrict these practices.

As an example, it was once possible to select from two methods of accounting following a takeover – merger accounting or acquisition accounting. The rules frequently allowed merger accounting to be adopted, which enabled reported earnings for the acquiring company to be boosted by including the full year's profits of a subsidiary acquired, even if it has been bought late in their financial year. Assets could be incorporated into the parent company's balance sheet at their existing balance sheet values rather than having to be revalued. In many cases this would have led to lower values for equipment, machinery, etc. Property would also have been substantially down-valued in the last five years.

A further example is the disguising of certain transactions by 'taking them through reserves' (see Trafalgar House case).

Illustration

Company balance sheet (£m)

Shareholders' funds:		Fixed assets	500
issued share capital	100	Current Assets	300
retained profit	500		
debt	200		
	800		800

If a business were acquired for £250m which had assets of £150m, the 'goodwill' or cost of control would be £100m.

There are three presentational choices:

- put £100m on the balance sheet as 'goodwill'
- write it off against current profits
- write it off against past profits, i.e. retained profits.

The first is difficult to support:

- is it a real asset?

- who says it is worth £100m? (Only the acquiring company which paid that price)
- if it had paid £500m for the same assets would this have made the combined company *more* valuable – or *less*?

The second choice would certainly not be popular – why penalise today's profits, making the existing business appear to be performing badly when the investment was made to create future profits?

The third option is painless. Few readers of financial statements will understand 'movements in reserves'. But has the high cost of an acquisition been disguised?

Higher standards of financial reporting demanded in the 1990s are making such practices more open. If an acquisition is disposed of, the goodwill previously written off has to be brought back to show the true profit or loss in the year. Taxation effects, for example, in carrying forward unrelieved losses can be a deciding factor in determining whether the value placed on an acquisition is financially justified.

KEY FINANCIAL DATA

Table 5.1

Performance indicator	Calculation	Information source
Profitability		
Return on sales	Earnings: sales	Profit statement
Return on capital employed	Earnings: total capital employed	Profit statement and position statement
Cash management		
Cash flow cover	Operating cash flow: dividend and interest payments	Cash flow statement
Free cash flow	Cash available for investment in the longer term growth of the business	Cash flow statement
Operational control		
Return on managed assets	Earnings: specific capital employed in a business unit	Segmental analyses
Capital structure		
Gearing	Debt: Equity	Position statement
Investment for the future	Cash spent	Cash flow statement

Assets	Information Source
Realisable values: Stock debtors	Position statement

Liabilities	
Short term creditors	Position statement and notes
Debt – Amounts, duration and rates	

Table 5.1 incorporates the major data that can be obtained from published financial statements. The earlier chapter (Chapter 1) on measuring business performance focused on interpreting data; the emphasis here is on valuation. A study of the accounting policies is needed for asset valuation roles and for profit recognition. The notes to the balance sheet will detail the debt amounts, currencies, maturities and interest rates. Future reporting standards will require covenant obligations and use of the growing array of financial instruments such as swaps, futures and options.

Study of the accounting policies will also help with the valuation of intangibles. Companies have been very keen to include brands as assets to strengthen their balance sheets, which in some cases has increased their borrowing potential. It also has had the effect of ensuring the company is fully valued on the basis of available information – no 'hidden assets'. An example is Guinness plc, which has a clearly defined policy contained in Note 13 to the 1993 accounts:

Acquired brands at cost
The amount stated for brands represents the cost of acquired brands. Brands are only recognised where title is clear, brand earnings are separately identifiable, the brand could be sold separately from the rest of the business and where the brand achieves earnings in excess of those achieved by unbranded products.

The cost of brands is calculated at acquisition, as part of the fair value accounting for businesses acquired, on the basis of after tax multiples of pre-acquisition earnings after deducting attributable capital employed.

The acquired brands which have been recognised include Bell's, Dewar's, Johnnie Walker, Old Parr and White Horse Scotch whiskies, Gordon's and Tanqueray gin and Asbach brandy.

The directors have reviewed the amounts at which brands are stated and are of the opinion that there has been no impairment in the value of the brands recognised, that all brands recognised could be sold for amounts substantially greater than those recognised in the balance sheet and that the end of the useful economic lives of the brands cannot be foreseen.

The sum of money involved is £1.395bn, representing 38 per cent of the total net assets. No home-grown brands are included in this figure, which was calculated at the date of acquisition. As a contrast, Rank Hovis McDougall has a different policy, described in Note 13 of its 1992 accounts:

The Group has valued its brands at the 'current use value to the Group', in conjunction with Interbrand Group plc, branding consultants.

This basis of valuation ignores any possible alternative use of a brand, any possible extension to the range of products currently marketed under a brand, any element of hope value and any possible increase in value of a brand due to either a special investment or a financial transaction (e.g. licensing) which would leave the Group with a different interest from the one being valued.

Intangible assets. The accounting treatment for additions to goodwill is considered on an individual basis and elimination against reserves has been selected as appropriate for the current year.

Brands, both acquired and created within the Group, are included at their 'current cost'. Such cost, which is reviewed annually, is not subject to amortisation.

WHAT IS THE RIGHT PRICE?

SPECTRUM OF VALUES

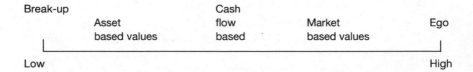

Figure 5.1

The value of anything is what someone is prepared to pay (see Field Group case). The practical approach is to prepare valuations resulting from many scenarios, concentrating on the key variables of:

- sales
- margins
- principal variable costs
- stepped fixed costs

The aim is to identify a 'cluster of valuations' arising from a number of valuation methods. This cluster will indicate a ball-park figure and become central in future negotiating. Ultimately the number in the box in the corner of Figure 5.2 will hold the answer to financial success of the acquired business.

WHAT IS THE RIGHT PRICE?

Costs
On-going financing:
 Interest payments
 Dividend payments

One time:
 Integration
 Capex catch-up

On-going operational:
 Management control

Benefits
Free cash flow

 +

Surplus asset
Sales proceeds

 +

Growth in
value of
the business

Figure 5.2

CHECKLIST OF ITEMS HELPFUL IN THE VALUATION PROCESS

Items of information		*Purpose/value in the process*
Trading history	→	to provide a perspective
Future plans in monetary terms	→	to enable the cash generation to be calculated
• prepared by the target company	→	optimistic, to raise the price?
• prepared by the acquiror	→	limited information concerned about over-optimistic projections level may be conservative or optimistic if the acquisition is much-wanted
• prepared by an independent experienced consultant	→	accustomed to the process ideally with specific industry knowledge hopefully unbiased and detached should be the most realistic
Up-to-date external valuation of principal assets, especially property	→	for the expert market opinion of the major saleable assets (sale/leaseback possibility)
Contingent liabilities:		
• Guarantee and warranty claims	→	to quantify potential future
• legal actions		liabilities
Profile of employees	→	to quantify potential future severance costs
• service contracts		
• length of service		
• conditions		

Items of information		*Purpose/value in the process*
• pension fund adequacy • actuarial projections	→	to enable assessment of: future liabilities potential contribution holiday, boosting profits recovery of surplus (difficult and unpopular)
Environmental impact survey of sites	→	to quantify potential future costs
Capex needed to equalise standards	→	to quantify the level of investment needed to ensure equality with existing facilities, enabling the benefits of flexibility and integration to be realised
Reason for sale of business	→	to identify 'distress sale' possibility and to use in the negotiating process
Terms of payment	→	to identify the options for financing and deferred payment and earn-out flexibility
Up-to-date current asset levels including aged analysis	→	to verify value and quality of stock and debtors
Details of future orders and contracts both placed and quoted	→	to assess future profitability and cash flows
Market share data	→	to help evaluate future pricing strategies
Details of long term supply contracts	→	to identify future contractual payments

Items of information		*Purpose/value in the process*
Distribution agreements	→	to calculate their value and any constraints affecting other parts of the business
Banking relationships and credit ratings	→	to highlight potential cost savings or value as sources of finance for other parts of business
Ownership structure and identity of shareholders	→	to identify potential strengths or weaknesses within the shareholder group as a help in the negotiating process
Differential voting rights for classes of shares	→	to assess the total value in relation to differential shareholder class rights

6

MANAGING SHORT TERM ASSETS AND LIABILITIES

CHAPTER OBJECTIVES
- To identify the components of working capital
- To describe techniques for minimising investment in working capital
- To stress the benefits of good financial housekeeping
- To examine specific operational decisions and their impact on working capital

The working capital of a business is the difference between the short term assets – mainly stock, debtors and cash – and the short term liabilities – largely supplier creditors, bank overdraft and taxes collected on behalf of the Government. Normally the value of the assets is greater than the liabilities, meaning the business has to finance this investment out of the long term funding. It is difficult to determine the optimum level of working capital for a specific business, which is influenced by several factors:

- **Nature of the business**
  - the need to provide a specified level of service
  - the requirement to maintain a range of goods.
- **Accepted trade practices**
  - industry payment norms – for example, the textile industry, with an accepted practice of settlement by the 10th of the month following to obtain discount, and garages that pay for petrol on delivery.

- Seasonal influences
  - Need to integrate manufacturing lead times with demand patterns.

PERFORMANCE MEASURES

Some business ratios help to determine the efficiency of working capital management by comparison with competitors and industry averages. The particularly relevant ones are:

Ratio **Description**
Stock holding days the number of days' sales (valued) at cost held in stock
Formula

$$\frac{\text{Closing stock} \times 360}{\text{Value of the materials content of cost of sales for the year}}$$

Ratio
Debtor days the number of days a business has to wait before receiving payment
Formula

$$\frac{\text{Closing debtors} \times 360}{\text{Total sales for the year}}$$

Ratio
Creditor days the number of days after delivery a business takes before it pays its suppliers
Formula

$$\frac{\text{Closing creditors} \times 360}{\text{Value of the materials content of cost of sales for the year}}$$

Negative working capital

It is possible in some businesses to have a negative working capital figure. This reduces the amount of long term investment necessary in the business and enables surplus cash to be invested short term to create interest income or, even longer term, to minimise the need to raise additional funds.

Businesses need good cash flow characteristics to produce this situation. Examples are:

- retailers – particularly those selling necessary and rapidly replaced goods such as food or newspapers
- suppliers of goods or services, such as construction companies, where payment of a deposit is an accepted practice
- mail order operations where cash is sent with order and delivery made at a later date.

MANAGING THE RESOURCES

Stock management

The quantity of stock held should be the minimum to maintain the promised customer service level. Techniques to enable this are the use of sophisticated computer systems such as MRP2, common component usage across models, centralised store locations and the 'just-in-time' concept.

The financial aspects of savings are:

- reduced interest cost on cash tied up in stock
- fewer materials handling costs
- lower cost of providing buildings and facilities
- less risk of obsolescence.

A trade-off between cost of stockholdings and cost of stock-outs if given in the tables below. Operating management control is vital in this area.

Costs of stockholding

- Providing buildings and facilities
- Insurance
- Risk of deterioration
- Risk of obsolescence
- Interest cost on cash tied up

Costs of stock-outs

- Loss of contribution towards profit
- Disrupted production and scheduling
- Loss of related business due to inadequate level of service
- Extra costs of providing higher specification of goods
- Extra costs of rapid restocking, e.g. distribution

Debtor management

Debtors are often the largest current asset in the balance sheet. They are also the area where the company has least control. They are interest-free loans to customers and the investment in them should be minimised. Until debtors pay there is a risk to the business of non-payment. A look at the aged debt profile – never shown in the published accounts – can be very revealing (see Table 6.1).

Table 6.1

	Balance sheet debtors figure @ 31.12.93	Aged debt profile 1993			
		December	November	October	September and earlier
Company A	£20m	£9m	£5.5m	£3.5m	£2m
Company B	£20m	£18m	£1m	£700,000	£300,000

The balance sheet debtors figure gives an identical picture for both companies. The real cash flow and risk position is substantially different when the aged debt profile is revealed. Company A has a lot of debt-checking to do, Company B can concentrate on the few problem customers.

Debtor vetting

Good debt management should start with credit vetting. This can be neglected if pressure is there to expand business and make deliveries or start contracts, but the cost in administration, financing and customer relationships will come, often as a hidden cost.

Standard techniques used for credit assessment

- **Contacting the potential customer's bank.** Banks are increasingly guarded in their responses to requests for credit references, and the selection of standardised replies can provide no more than a level of either comfort or discomfort.
- **Asking regular trade suppliers to give their views.** Recent payment history in normal trading should be the best guide to how a new customer would operate the account. It is too easy for a business to have a small number of supplier accounts that they consistently pay within terms, perhaps even taking discounts. This pool of credit reference may not be entirely representative and again can only contribute towards a view.
- **Checking with credit rating agencies such as Dunn & Bradstreet**. Credit rating agencies are a professional, regularly

updated source of information. They incur a cost dependent on the level of detail requested. As a guideline they must have a place, although they are dependent on the quality of information provided for their analysis. It is very easy for a busy financial/credit controller to respond to a credit enquiry with a fairly bland comment such as 'normally within terms'.

Requesting recent financial reports

This helps to give an overall picture, but the most recent set will be some months out of date and of very limited value for analysis of short term liquidity.

The dilemma of making the final decision

Granting credit is a risk decision. It is not the biggest or the longest term decision, but it could be the most common. There will have to be an acceptance of a level of risk to ensure that normal trading can continue. The decision to seize an order because of the additional sales volume and profitability will be wrong if no cash is received.

What else can we do?

- **Deposits/payment in advance.** Not a popular way to start a customer and supplier relationship, but it can be taken as a gesture of good faith and a measure of financial stability. The risk level to the supplier is reduced.
- **Direct debit arrangements.** From the credit control point of view, this is the perfect arrangement, beaten only by payment in advance. Cash is received automatically and attention can be focused quickly on problem accounts. The quicker that action is taken, the lower the risk and level of loss.
- **Professional links.** Credit controllers within an industry may be able to share some commercial information in the best interests of their company. They should maintain strong links with their sales colleagues in particular, who accumulate useful trade information in their day-to-day jobs.
- **Sales commission arrangements.** It can help in reducing bad debt

levels if commission payments are made only on *paid* sales invoices. This should not only help to reduce the initial risk but also ensure quicker cash flow.

- **Late filing of accounts.** There is some evidence that companies which file accounts with public authorities late or only just within statutory periods are often experiencing liquidity problems. This does not apply to subsidiaries of publicly quoted groups where the aim is simply to delay publishing commercial information that may be of value to competitors.

The final credit decision

It is a policy decision to accept some level of risk. Losses will have to be met by other sales customers, ultimately as part of the margin. A comparative summary is given below of the costs allowing deferred payment and the costs of *not* allowing it.

Costs of allowing deferred payment

- Lost interest (until value received)
- Loss of purchasing power in an inflationary period
- Credit assessment
- Account handling/monitoring
- Bad debt or insurance
- Discount – although it will reduce some of the above (but it is a reduced margin)

Costs of *not* allowing deferred payment

- Goodwill
- Competitive disadvantage
- Inconvenience and security cost of cash handling

Cash management

The key objectives are:

- **Liquidity.** The company must have cash facilities available to meet payments as agreed. A secondary objective would be to do this at overall minimum cost.
- **Safety.** Investment of short term surplus cash should be as profitable as possible with a high level of security and access.

Cash forecasting

To enable the key objectives to be satisfied it will be necessary to forecast cash flows in advance so that borrowing or investing arrangements can be made. The criteria to be assessed are:

- the cash inflows anticipated from routine trading
- special inflows, e.g. asset sale proceeds
- committed cash outflows
- for surplus amounts – the period they are available for investment
- for deficit amounts – the period for which they will need to be financed.

Investing the surplus

If a company consistently has cash greater than its predictable needs there is a strong argument that it is not maximising the returns from the business. The returns from pure no-risk cash investment should be lower than the return on capital employed achieved by the business. If this is not the case then the cash should be distributed to shareholders as a special dividend. An example, for a different reason, of paying a special dividend see the London Weekend Television case. An alternative to dividend distribution is to examine ways of investing in the business development of the company with the aim of increasing future shareholder value.

The aforementioned options are better for long term investment. The alternatives described below are all for the short term, defined as under a year.

Investment alternatives

- **Bank deposit accounts.** These are only appropriate for small amounts of cash for short periods. They may have specific features such as instant availability and differential rates for larger deposits. The more flexibility required, the lower the rates, which are fixed by individual banks influenced by market rates.
- **Money market deposits.** Generally they give better rates, but there is a minimum deposit of £250,000 and a notice period for access to funds is required – normally seven days. The rate of interest is more market-driven. Sophisticated cash forecasting is required to manage this process effectively.
- **Certificates of deposit (CD).** These can be purchased from banks. They give a slightly lower return than other deposits but are negotiable instruments. This means that they can be bought and sold on a secondary market, which enables them to be turned back into cash very quickly. The rates can be fixed or variable so there is a potential capital gain or loss, and credit risk attaches to the issuing bank. They are an extremely popular investment medium in the US, where they are also issued by commercial organisations.
- **Commercial paper.** This is short term (maximum 364 days) debt issued by a corporate business. It is a negotiable instrument and credit assessment is an important part of the investment decision. Ratings are an increasingly common guide to the creditworthiness of this type of investment, helping to quantify the risk-return relationship.

Creditor management

Careful use of creditor funding provides short term interest-free finance to a business. The easy answer is not simply to hang on to the cash for as long as possible. Stretching the patience of a supplier beyond its limit can cause very large, often hidden, costs. Production delays and disruption due to materials shortages, purchasing small quantities at higher prices to ensure supply, additional in-brand and out-bound distribution costs and using a higher grade or quality of material than specified are common examples.

UK companies are slow to pay their bills compared with those of many other European countries (see Table 6.2). Although 30 days is a commonly accepted contractual period, a typical period in the UK is 78 days. This compares with 48 days in Germany, Sweden and Norway.

Table 6.2

	Denmark	Ireland	UK	Italy	France	Germany	Switzerland
Average debt days	50	60	78	89	104	45	45

Source: Intrum Justitia Survey

Integrating the management of stock debtors and cash

The management of both debtors and creditors is increasingly being incorporated into more rigid contractual agreements for larger companies and regular suppliers. It is clear in the long run that companies can only pay their bills from the money they receive from customers. Unacceptable levels of borrowing to fund the gap will cause margins to be eroded, prices to be uncompetitive or ultimately force the closure of the business.

Financing debtors

A source of debtor finance is to sell the debts to a third party which effectively lends cash until payment is available. There are immediate cash flow benefits, but it is an expensive source of funds, reflecting the level of risks. It is used mainly by small and medium sized companies.

Financing stock

Stock can be held on consignment or sale or return bases to minimise investment by the customer. This could have financial benefit for a supplier in saving storage and handling costs. A specific illustration where a supplier can gain extra business is when the supply is to a retailer. In a retail outlet there is a chance of making a sale, in a supply warehouse there is none. A high level of demand could generate more orders. The problem on the other side is the return of unsold out-of-season goods.

SUMMARY

Understandably, great emphasis is placed on the major decisions in a business – such as raising long term finance, making capital invest- ments and acquisitions. These decisions are taken at a strategic level in the organisation. Decisions on financing and investment in short term assets have to be made by operating managers with their local know- ledge. It is important that good financial housekeeping is targeted, practised and monitored continuously. Mistakes here may not be as disastrous individually as wrong strategic decisions, but collectively the result can be equally catastrophic.

7

MAKING OPERATIONAL FINANCIAL DECISIONS

CHAPTER OBJECTIVES

- To provide a background to the financial decisions made by operating managers
- To examine the financial aspects of:
  - the pricing decision
  - the out-sourcing decision
  - customer and product profitability analysis

Managers at the operating level in a business make decisions every day which have an impact on company profitability, cash flow and levels of investment. Although the core of making many business decisions is finance, there are many other internal and external factors surrounding the numbers (see Figure 7.1).

Strategy defines the broad direction of the business, operational tactics determine the precise route and pace. There is a need to understand the way the internal finances of a business operate and how they interface with external financial management. Understanding the cost structure and behaviour of the business will enable better operational decisions to be made.

Three key operating decisions have been selected to illustrate the analysis and techniques in existence to help the decision-making process:

- pricing
- out-sourcing
- customer and product profitability analysis.

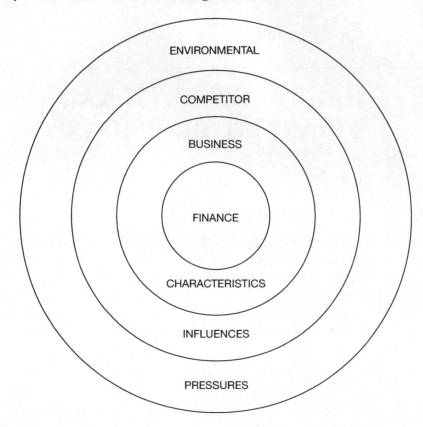

Figure. 7.1

None of these decisions can be taken on a purely financial basis. They are about improving the profit performance of the business, which must work through to cash. Sometimes the benefits will be non-financial and difficult to quantify. Often they will be perceived as decisions to be made by non-accountants. Today we have to look *across* the business not *down* functional silos.

THE PRICING DECISION

The factors which influence the pricing decision are displayed in Figure 7.2, with the impact of timescale shown in Figure 7.3. Ultimately the decision has to incorporate the varying influences of the factors on the type of product.

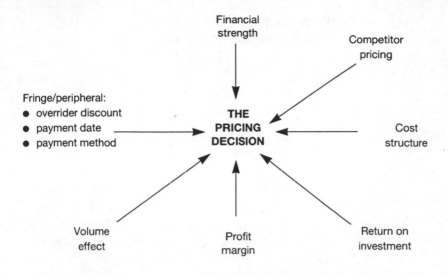

Figure 7.2

Where the product or service is aimed at a niche market, usually with some specialist or differentiated characteristics, competitor prices are less relevant. Where the product or service is at the commodity end of the spectrum, aimed at the mass market, volume is the key influence and competitor prices are more relevant.

Any pricing strategy and technique (see Table 7.1) may only be appropriate for a limited time and for specific products or services.

**THE IMPACT OF TIMESCALE ON
THE PRICING DECISION**

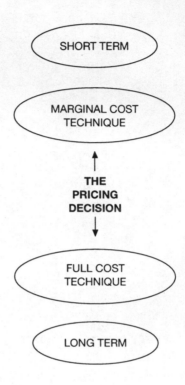

Figure 7.3

Table 7.1   Pricing strategies and techniques

Strategies	Techniques
Internal cost-based	Absorption cost
	Marginal cost
	Cost plus
External market or competition based	Skimming
	Penetration
	Perceived value
	Broader concept

Internal cost-based strategies

Absorption cost (also known as full cost)

The principle here is that it is essential to recover all the costs of the business from the projected output. The profit required can be treated just like any other cost.

SUITABLE SITUATIONS

- Where there is a delivery lead time created and supported by a full order book.
- Where the demand is predictable and continuous, enabling a volume assumption to be made.
- Where the product or service is clearly differentiated from the competition, or substitutes are perceived to be 'just not the same'.

DRAWBACKS

- Entirely dependent on selling the projected volume.
- Ignores the market.
- Price too low – missed opportunity to maximise profit.
- Price too high – failure to sell predicted volume.

TYPICAL APPLICATIONS

This strategy is used in many businesses where time is still the main determinant of output, for example engineering, where each job is different, shipbuilding and maintenance and servicing charges for equipment.

Marginal cost

- This is based on the contribution concept, which measures costs in two ways: fixed – those necessary to support the operation even if only producing a single item – and variable – the pure additional cost incurred for each additional item produced. If the product or service is priced over the variable cost the excess is called contribution. When the total contribution is equal to the fixed cost this is called the break even point. Beyond that, it is profit.

SUITABLE SITUATIONS

Where the business is operating beyond break even point but the fixed costs are at a level to support greater activity, i.e. there is spare capacity.

DRAWBACKS

- If all business is achieved by pricing in this way very large volumes are needed to achieve profitability.
- If the products are perceived to be the same the business may be competing with itself at lower margins, leading to cannibalism.

TYPICAL APPLICATIONS

Own label – where the product is produced for another brand label, typically that of a major retailer.

Cost plus

This used to be one of the main methods used for pricing Government contracts. The aim was to restrict and control the profitability. The principle is simple. A detailed schedule of costs relevant to the particular contract or service is prepared, the agreed profit percentage (commonly 5 per cent) is added and that becomes the price.

SUITABLE SITUATIONS

Where an essential service was being provided and considerations of quality, availability, continuity and possibly secrecy were judged to be more important than price alone.

DRAWBACKS

- Inefficient
  It could perpetuate inefficiency by protecting a high cost-base. It was in the interests of the supplier to increase costs as much as possible as a greater cost led to a greater profit due to the percentage uplift.
- Fraud
  It requires a combination of technical understanding, business

awareness and financial and auditing skills to safeguard against fraud.

APPLICATIONS

- Used particularly for defence contracts where the Government was the only domestic customer, where secrecy was critical and often the product was under development, and in some cases may not have been technically possible.
- Cost plus has recently come back to popularity; it has been used for distribution contracts – but very 'open book' and carefully controlled.

External market based

Skimming

This is pricing at the highest possible level at which customers will buy, often achieved by a shortage – artificially created or real – and by stressing the superiority in some way of the product. Price has to be moved down when sales start to plateau, either because all those who want to buy have bought or the competition is attacking.

SUITABLE SITUATIONS

- Where a state-of-the-art technical product is introduced.
- Where large development and pilot production costs have been incurred, skimming has the merit of providing useful sizeable cash inflows early in the life of the product.
- Where capacity is limited, either deliberately or unavoidably.

DRAWBACKS

Size of market – the initial sales are inevitably restricted as only the top-end of the market is being targeted.

COMPETITION

If high margins look achievable many competitors are going to be attracted, which will force prices down *unless* there are clearly differentiated factors.

TYPICAL APPLICATIONS

- The introduction of the CD player, where a clear image was created of a distinctly superior product in terms of sound quality, ease of use, durability and greater capacity. A high-price strategy was adopted and as competition entered at lowest prices the reaction was to match or differentiate, *but* by this time economies of scale were beginning to come through.
- The high-definition television (HDTV) has the potential to be introduced with a similar pricing strategy.

Penetration

This is almost the reverse of skimming. Here a low-price strategy is adopted with the aim of dominating the market, taking advantage of huge volume sales. Although contribution per unit may be low, the volume effect will create a large total figure. This has the effect of frightening potential competition, which worries about how it can attract the volume sales which it needs given the competitive pricing structure.

SUITABLE SITUATIONS

Where a new mass market exists and huge volumes can be generated very quickly.

DRAWBACKS

- Sales volume
  If the sales are not achieved, huge losses are almost inevitable.
- Future profitability
  Having created effectively a commodity product, profitability improvements are hard to achieve.

Perceived value

Potentially the best strategy of all because it is the closest to the customer in fixing a price that is 'perceived' to be value for money *to the buyer*.

SUITABLE SITUATIONS

Perceived value applies in many purchasing situations but is more appropriate where there is a need to persuade the buyer to spend more for fundamentally the same product or to have the same utility.

TYPICAL APPLICATIONS

Product	**Substitute**
• LAMY pen	Biro
• IBM computer	'clone'
• Filofax	diary
• Tag Heuer/Seiko	Casio digital watch

Broader concept

This brings together many of the strategies described earlier. The principle is to provide the customer with a product or service which to him has a greater value than the cost of providing it.

SUITABLE SITUATIONS

Where the incremental cost of providing is very low and additional sales or use might occur which would otherwise not have happened.

DRAWBACKS

There are no significant ones, particularly as the product or service supplied has a low variable cost.

TYPICAL APPLICATIONS

• Two for the price of one.
• Lower price telephone calls to a long-distance area.
• Software packages – licence agreements.

Summary

No pricing strategy is appropriate where costs are not covered in the long term and only in limited controlled circumstances in the short term. But we have to sell in the market. The following may be an old saying but it is still true: 'You have to have the right product in the right place at the right price.'

One recent example of a short term pricing strategy has been the newspaper price war in the UK, led by News International. The end of recession and a balance sheet showing improving financial strength have enabled price cutting to take place. There are few forecasts of how long it will last or how many casualties will result.

THE OUT-SOURCING DECISION

A major business sector enjoying considerable growth in the past decade has been the provision of services, ranging from security, catering and cleaning through equipment hire to specialist services such as computer maintenance and temperature-controlled distribution. The motive behind this has been the vogue of 'sticking to the knitting': concentrating on the core business, leaving services to be handled by dedicated providers.

There are non-financial factors involved in making the decision to move to an external service provider, such as:

- quality
- reliability
- viability of having sufficient demand for a service, particularly an in-house one
- elimination of the 'hassle' factor.

The ultimate driver of the decision is going to be cost, influenced by specific factors such as those above. The determination of real internal cost savings has been the subject of great debate. Establishing the alternative external contract cost is easy, determining its quality and reliability is very difficult.

Direct costs are easily determined. The main costs and the consequence of decision to out-source are given below:

Direct costs	Out-sourcing consequence
Salaries and on-cost • Social taxes • Pension funding	Long term saving. Short term cost – redundancy payment
Premises occupancy • Business rates • Opportunity cost of rental or income from sale proceeds • Insurance • Heating, lighting and power • Building repairs and maintenance	Entirely dependent on specific situation; maybe total saving for example specialist vehicle maintenance carried out off-site or equally could be no saving at all as the facilities are still owned, maintained and used and the out-sourcing is only of facilities management
Management savings	An illusory concept – is there really a reduction in these costs? But there may be a benefit from focusing attention on the core business.
Equipment used • May be leased	Is sub-lease possible?
• Who is responsible for maintenance? • Who is responsible for capital replacement?	Are either of these possible when separated from ownership?

Additional costs

You have to ask whether there is an extra cost for monitoring the quality and reliability of the service and a greater risk and reliance on external providers which could be reflected in higher costs in the future.

Non-financial elements

Internally the level of service quality is easily apparent. Quantifying a reduction in service level is difficult. Attempting to calculate the cost of returning to an in-house operation is extremely hard and may even be a practical impossibility. The ability to focus on the core business has a distinct benefit. The service provider ought to be able to bring some efficiency and economies of scale gains which will not be available to the out-sourcer. The ultimate decision is going to be based on consideration of all the factors, but short term cash flow improvement has a tempting appeal for many businesses.

Illustration

An interesting effect of an out-sourced service can be found in the prepared-food industry. This sector has experienced explosive growth in the last decade due to the expanding market, resulting from changing social habits, and the availability of capacity created by suppliers seeking to exploit the economies of scale. The latter has led to some very attractive pricing for the out-sourcer as a result of a marginal pricing approach used by the supplier. Often the ingredients and packaging are supplied, which enables tight quality control, and distribution is normally contracted out. The out-sourced service is therefore restricted to the labour and use of machinery needed to complete the processing of the food.

Food is clearly part of the FMCG (fast-moving consumer goods) sector. Rapidly changing, perhaps even temporary, demands of customers can open up a potential profit opportunity – but can the out-sourced supplier respond? This decision is based on two factors:

- the availability of processing capacity
- the maximising of profitability by processing the products which produce the greatest margins.

It is highly likely that if the first is restricted, the own brand will produce the higher margins.

If the flexibility to increase volumes is desired, the argument about moving from a marginal cost pricing basis to a full cost basis will open up, quoting higher maintenance costs resulting from increased plant utilisation as a basis for higher prices.

Commercial negotiations restart!

CUSTOMER AND PRODUCT PROFITABILITY ANALYSIS

The drive to reduce costs has become an endemic part of corporate life. No longer is it an exercise to be carried out and recuperated from afterwards; it has developed into a continuous activity. The search for cost reduction has led to an analysis of every aspect of cost and the questioning of the value delivered. In the end we all work for our customers – without them there is no one to pay our salaries. They probably pay us more for our better products and we ought to sell as many of those as possible. This leaves us with some questions to answer:

- Who are our best customers?
- Which are our best products?

In both cases 'best' means most profitable, which enables us to generate the maximum cash flow for reinvestment and rewarding our investors. It does not mean largest or favourite.

How do we identify the most profitable customers and products? We have to start with *cost* and identify what is meant by that word. The increasing use of automated processes has reduced the proportion of the product or service cost attributed to direct labour to typically around 5 per cent of total costs. A comparison with manufacturing industry in the 1960s would have produced a comparable figure of 60 per cent. The proportion of direct material costs to total costs has fallen equally sharply. Traditional methods of overhead apportionment and absorption have often relied upon labour hours or material cost as the basis. In many instances neither of these are appropriate as they no longer are influencing or 'driving' the cost.

A technique used increasingly to identify the cost drivers is ABC – Activity Based Costing. It aims to align organisational (indirect overhead) costs with operational activity to enable costs to be accumulated around a product or service. The approach is to focus on what is *generating* the cost rather than merely to allocate it. The first stage in the

ABC process is to perform an activity analysis in each overhead area and then measure what causes each activity to occur.

Illustration – Handling a potential new client in a management development consultancy

Cost activity and driver analysis

Activity	Cost driver
Contact potential client	Marketing manager
Research client background	Research facility
Initial meeting on-site	Marketing and client manager
Follow up meeting on client's premises	Client manager
Preparation and submission of proposal	Client manager
Client manager to present and discuss proposal	Client manager
Detailed programme design and development	Client manager and tutors
Run pilot programme	Facilities charges and tutor time
Evaluate tutor and delegate feedback	Client manager and tutor
Final programme design	Client manager and tutor time
Commence series of programmes	Facilities charges and tutor time
Update content regularly	Tutor time
Continue existing programme development	Client manager and tutor time
Start discussions for further initiatives	Client manager

This analysis reveals that the principal cost drivers are:

Activity	Cost driver
Customer handling	Client manager
Programme teaching	Tutor
Programme facilities	Facilities charges

It is possible to work out the real costs by spreading the total costs of the client manager and tutor time in line with their input. Facilities charges can be recovered on a per capita basis and fees charges by marketing and research on a cost basis (for database searches) plus an hourly charge-out rate. Client profitability can be determined using these costs and specific client income. Product profitability can be calculated using the same technique.

The use of the technique can be taken more widely and encompasses other techniques such as zero based budgeting, where each budget cost-head starts with zero and has to be justified. The total concept has become known as Activity Based Management (ABM) or Value Based Management (VBM) and has linked with Total Quality Management (TQM) and Business Process Re-engineering.

Summary

The job of management is increasingly about allocating scarce resources through the business effectively, to generate the largest cash flows. Activity Based Management is a tool to help this process as it ensures a clear understanding of costs and how they relate to activities.

8

MANAGING MONEY INTERNATIONALLY

CHAPTER OBJECTIVES

- To provide a background to the importance of international finance, particularly in handling currency flows
- To identify the types of risk involved in trading in different currencies
- To outline the techniques for managing currency risks
- To provide a framework for selecting appropriate techniques in specific business situations
- To produce an outline and illustration of the use of the main financial derivatives

---

B usiness has become increasingly international and companies cannot ignore the effect of currency changes on cash flow, profitability and overall position of the company. No company is wholly immune. Exports are affected by the value of the home currency in relation to other trading partners. Raw material imports affect production costs; finished product imports are often competitors in the domestic market. The risks extend beyond the trading sphere. Finance is a global industry and companies borrow and invest in many currencies. It is not sufficient that only financial people understand how currency risks are created and managed.

The 1990s have brought regular corporate casualties involving major losses from some aspect of foreign currency dealings or the use of financial derivatives or instruments. In 1991 it was Allied Lyons (see case) that suffered the biggest ever loss in foreign exchange dealings incurred by a UK company. The £150m figure resulted from 'dealing in foreign currency instruments which were inappropriate, and in which it lacked the requisite trading skills' as the Chairman reported on 4 May 1991. Although long term damage to the company was avoided, both the Chairman and the Finance Director are no longer employed by the company. In 1992 Showa Shell reported a Y115.3bn ($1.09bn) loss from $4.6bn worth of dollars futures contracts used mainly for purchasing crude oil. During 1993 Metallgesellschaft (see case), the mining metals and industrial group, hit liquidity problems arising out of dealings in oil futures. The losses from these transactions eventually exceeded Dm2.25bn.

Understanding the risks involved is important in helping to decide how to manage them and the best techniques and instruments to use.

WHAT ARE THE RISKS?

Currency risk is the net potential effect of exchange rate movements on the profit and loss account and the balance sheet of the company. The currency risks faced by a business can be grouped under three headings:

- transaction risk
- translation risk
- economic strategic or competitive risk.

Transaction risk

This risk involves exchange rate movements that affect the value of foreign currency flows. It is the only risk which has a direct cash effect and arises when a transaction is entered into and requires an actual conversion from one currency to another. The most common situation will be the sale or purchase of goods or services invoiced on credit terms in foreign currencies. Another common risk or exposure arises when interest or dividends are paid or received. This type of risk is either historic or predictable and easily quantified, making the protection or 'hedging' process straightforward. Successful management of currency risks or 'exposures' needs to cope with transactions that have not yet been identified but are likely to occur.

Price list exposure

An exporting company publishes a price list in a local currency. It is commercially impractical to change prices in less than six months. Actual transaction exposure only arises when a foreign currency invoice is issued. This actual exposure lasts until payment is received and converted into the domestic currency. The need to consider managing exposures starts with the issue of the price list, and some hedging may be necessary to protect the company against loss.

Capital expenditure exposure

Capital expenditure is often planned and committed over a long period. There may be no actual transaction exposure until purchase contracts are awarded, but if the project is dependent on them there is an exposure which in this case can be identified and quantified.

Tender to contract exposure

A company regularly submitting tenders for the supply of goods or services has the trading process displayed in Figure 8.1.

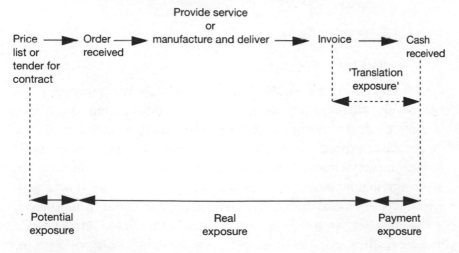

TRANSACTION RISK

When does the currency exposure arise?

Figure 8.1

Translation risk

Translation risk arises when amounts fixed in foreign currency are converted to domestic equivalents for financial reporting purposes. There is no immediate cash effect. Translation can affect both the profit and loss statement and the balance sheet. Broadly similar accounting standards exist in the US and UK, and the consensus treatment is to convert profits or losses for a foreign subsidiary at an average exchange rate over the accounting period and to convert assets and liabilities at a period-end rate.

Profit and loss statement translation

The profit and loss translation is only a paper figure initially but may become a 'real' transaction exposure if cash interest or dividend needs to be paid. A company with major non-UK income but a high proportion of UK-based costs can have a problem with translation but use techniques to minimise the transaction effect.

The other impact occurs where the reported profitability is so reduced that either the market value of the company or its borrowing ability is affected. The market value of a company should be an assessment of its future worth. Shareholders need to be kept well informed and persuaded that short term currency fluctuations are not good indicators of long term shareholder value.

Balance sheet translation

The foreign currency assets of the business are not exposed in real terms unless they are for sale and the intention is to remit cash back to a home country. Liabilities denominated in foreign currencies do represent a real exposure in the future if they are repayable loans.

The impact of translation on gearing has to be evaluated and checked to ensure that no covenants are breached, even if only technically. An obvious way around this problem is to match the investment in foreign currency assets with debt denominated in equivalent currencies. The practical difficulty here is how far the company will go to protect *reported* earnings and incur a cost that will affect the bottom line. It is also possible that a real transaction exposure is created by a currency borrowing.

Economic strategic or competitive risk

Economic exposure covers the indirect risk to the profitability and cash flow of the company that would arise from changes in exchange rates. It represents the early stages of transaction exposure. The timing and amount of the cash flows are uncertain or even completely unknown; as the situation progresses and more data becomes available it ceases to be an economic exposure and becomes a transaction exposure. Economic exposure covers some of the pre-transactional risks such as tender to contract, price list and capital expenditure exposures.

MANAGING CURRENCY RISKS

A range of techniques exists which enables companies to limit their exposure to the effect of fluctuating exchange rates. The decision to protect or 'hedge' is made after an assessment of the significance of the risk to the business of exchange rate movements. The choice of hedging technique should be made when sufficient expertise exists in the business to determine the correct one for the specific situation in the business, following an assessment of the impact on business of the following factors:

- the percentage of the company's turnover which is exposed to currency risk
- the individual size of a single exposure
- the market position of the company and its resultant ability to use commercial techniques to react to competitive pressures
- the portfolio of currencies in which the company trades and whether there are potential off-setting transactions
- the relationship of costs to sales within trading blocks, e.g. ERM currencies, USD Group – USA, Canada, Hong Kong, Malaysia, Singapore, Saudi Arabia, Deutsche Mark Group (outside the ERM) Austria, Switzerland, Finland, Sweden, Republic of Ireland (more loosely related)

- the ability to 'match' the currency of sales with that of costs
- the previous experience of the company in relation to foreign exchange trading and its own forecasting record
- the level of currency management expertise within the business
- the flexibility of the company to withdraw from specific markets and obtain alternative profitable business
- the overall level of profitability and financial strength of the business.

Techniques can be split into two groups:

- internal
- external.

Internal

Sometimes known as commercial or natural, this group of techniques involves taking action within the business. Examples are:

Pricing

- In the currency where the majority of the **costs** are incurred.
- In the domestic currency of the main **competitors** so that comparative prices are unaffected by exchange rate change.
- Inserting an exchange rate variation clause to protect profit margins from the implications of changes in the exchange rate.

Matching

- Set up an equal and opposite commercial transaction at the time the original exposure is generated, e.g. buying raw materials with a currency receivable.
- Or borrow in a currency to finance an asset purchase.

Netting

- Used as an alternative to matching, when only a part of the original exposure can be 'matched', leaving a 'net' amount still exposed, but reducing the overall risk.

Leading and lagging

- Simply either delaying payment or settling early in anticipation of falling or rising exchange rates.
- This method is safe, simple to manage and cheap.

Inter-company payment discipline

- Inter-company payables and receivables are 'real' exposures.
- Complying with payment terms limits exposures to the short term.
- Inter-company settlement should rank equally with external liabilities. The currency exposure is identical.
- There is no cancelling gain and loss situation within a group. When the transaction interacts with the market there will be a gain *or* loss – and it will be *real*.

Illustration

A German media company with an Italian subsidiary invoices in Deutschmarks. If the lire devalues, the Italian company will have to find more lire to pay the Deutschmark invoice and there will be a real transaction loss, with no gain for the German company, which is receiving Deutschmarks in payment of a Deutschmark invoice. If the invoice were in lire the German company would make the loss instead of the Italian company but it would be of the same size and affect the group identically.

Withdrawal from the market

- The contract should contain a clause which allows withdrawal from the market when returns have reached an unacceptable level, with no residual legal liability.

External

The use of external techniques needs to be evaluated when internal techniques have been considered and used where possible. There are four main instruments:

- forward contracts
- lending and borrowing
- options
- swaps.

Forward contracts

A forward transaction is an agreement to exchange a fixed amount of one currency for a fixed amount of another currency at an agreed date in the future. The effective exchange rate is derived from the comparative interest rates of the two currencies being exchanged. Its suitability depends on being able to forecast the currency flows confidently. If the forecast proves not to be accurate the business has in reality **created** an exposure rather than **protected** an existing one because the forward contract is a binding agreement to deliver a quantity of one currency and receive a quantity of another. The key features of a forward contract are:

- certainty
- simplicity } enabling good cash management
- off balance sheet – it does not count as borrowings affecting the **gearing**
- normally sourced from a bank.

Lending and borrowing

As an alternative to a forward contract the currency could be exchanged immediately in the *spot* market i.e. where the transaction is agreed on the 'spot' and takes place immediately. The exchange rate is known and fixed, the transaction immediate (two days delivery normally) and the administration and monitoring of forward contracts are avoided. The currency is normally deposited in an interest bearing currency account until needed.

Illustration

A forward transaction to buy yen for a capital equipment purchase has been made. Delivery will be late. A way around this problem would be to take delivery of the yen as agreed and put them on deposit until needed. As the yen interest rates are lower than sterling there will be an effective interest cost. If delivery were available earlier and agreed to by the company, yen could be borrowed short term and repaid when the forward contract matured.

Financial derivatives? Options – currency and commodity

An option is the **right** but not the **obligation** to exchange a fixed amount of one currency for a fixed amount of another within, or at the end of, a pre-determined period. In effect it is a forward contract that can be walked away from, where you lose only the cost of the option, which could be 3–5 per cent of the contract value. It therefore has the advantage of limiting the down-side as the maximum cost is known at the beginning, whilst leaving unlimited profit potential. These options are ideally suited to transactions, where the size or existence of the exposure is uncertain, for example tender-to-contract or price list exposures.

Illustration

A commodity option

A quantity of a commodity (or currency to pay for it) is needed in three months' time. A dealer is willing to accept $100 per tonne to supply a predetermined quantity at $2,000 per tonne. If the price of this commodity in three months' time is $1,700 per tonne then the option would be thrown away, the product bought in the spot market and the cost to the company would be $1,800 per tonne. The tender-to-contract or price list item would have been safeguarded and the price could even be reduced by $200 per tonne if competitive conditions demanded. If the price of the commodity rose, the company's cost would be contained. The option could be sold at a profit if the product was not needed or the loss would in any event be limited to $100 per tonne.

There are two types of option:

- **calls** – giving the right to buy a currency
- **puts** – giving the right to sell a currency.

Currency options

The exchange rate (known as the strike price) and the expiry date of the option are chosen by the customer at the outset. The cost (known as the premium) of the option is calculated based on these decisions and the volatility of the currency involved. Options can be exchange-traded, where they exist in standardised form, or over-the-counter, where they are written to fit a customer's particular circumstances.

There are two styles of option:

- **American option**. The buyer can 'exercise' the option – make the exchange of currencies – at any time up to the expiry date or let it lapse.
- **European option**. This can only be exercised on the expiry date and is slightly cheaper because of its lack of flexibility.

Options may have a resale value determined by the same criteria as the original cost. When the exercise price of an option is better than the current spot exchange rate it is called 'in the money' – when it is the other way around it is 'out of the money'.

Swaps

Swaps are like long-dated forward contracts. They involve the exchange of a liability now with the exchange back at a pre-determined future time and the compensation of the other party for costs in the intervening period. Swaps are used primarily to protect an investment or portfolio of borrowings. They involve a back-to-back loan between companies with a matching but opposite need. What is 'swapped' is essentially a series of cash flows.

Ilustrations of a way to use a swap

A UK company wishes to raise cash to invest in developing its business in the US. It is quoted in the UK only, which means it does not have access to US capital markets and does not have a rating, which would make it extremely difficult to borrow in the US.

What sources of funds are available?

- Raise equity via a UK rights issue.

- Borrow sterling from a UK bank.
- Borrow in $.

The first two of these options will appear on a balance sheet as £sterling liabilities, but the asset will appear as $ assets, creating a translation exposure. The returns from the investment will be in $, which will create a translation exposure as they are converted to £ income in the profit statement, and a transaction exposure as they need to be converted to pay £sterling interest or dividend.

A solution is to 'swap' the currency flows for the duration of a loan, paying or receiving a sum of money from the other party leaving both sides in an equivalent cash flow position but having avoided specific payments in another currency. The loan would revert to the borrowing currency upon maturity.

Figure 8.2 diagrammatically illustrates how a hedging technique can be selected.

SELECTING A HEDGING TECHNIQUE
FOR A CURRENCY RISK

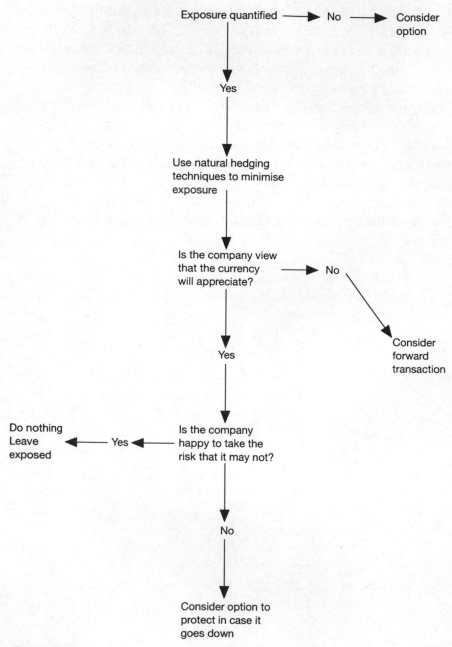

Figure 8.2

9

ENHANCING SHAREHOLDER VALUE

CHAPTER OBJECTIVES

- To explain the concept of shareholder value
- To describe the factors that contribute to creating shareholder value
- To illustrate the practical applications of the concept
- To outline a practical framework for achieving the objective of creating shareholder value
- To list the advantages of shareholder value as a better means of evaluating corporate performance for shareholders than traditional profit-based measures such as earnings per share

Corporate executives are rarely pleased with the price of the company's stock. If it is low, which can usually be defined as appreciably below a peak level recently achieved, they make comments like 'undervalued' and 'not understood by the market'. If it is high, usually defined as the highest price achieved recently, they worry about expectations being too high, about falling investment return yields and how to maintain the high rating awarded by the market.

Concern about a possible takeover bid can stem from both a low and a high stock price. A low price causes the fear that stockholders will be dissatisfied and sell, possibly causing further price falls. A high price can mean rising expectations or active buying by a potential predator. In the UK there is a compulsory disclosure when the holding reaches 3 per cent, or 1 per cent during a takeover bid. Other European countries have similar rules and some restrict the level of ownership by an individual holder. In Switzerland, for example, most companies restrict a single shareholding to 5 per cent, while in Spain 10 per cent is common.

Shareholders have worries as well. They invest in ordinary shares (common stock) for two reasons: to receive cash dividend income and to share in the growth in value of the business in the form of a capital gain, realisable in cash when the investment is sold. Thus the main flow for shareholders' attention is cash.

Much of the financial information available to investors concentrates on the past, yet returns will only come in the future. Profitability is often the centre of financial reporting but can be greatly affected by accounting policy changes and differences. Earnings per share statistics are derived from profit, not cash. It is important that financial reporting stresses cash flow to link with the expectations of shareholders.

THE CONCEPT OF SHAREHOLDER VALUE

The concept is based on the premise that shareholders seek their returns from investment in cash – either short term in the form of dividend, or deferred in the form of a capital gain coming from a higher share price. In order to deliver value to the shareholders, companies need to maximise future cash flows from the portfolio of businesses. There are implications for operating company managers in having to evaluate both the operating performance and the terminal value of the business unit in net present value terms.

An essential number for these calculations is the cost of capital for the company. By discounting cash flows from individual business units at the overall cost of capital the potential shareholder value can be derived. If this total exceeds the market capitalisation of the business then the shareholders' wealth would be maximised by 'unbundling' (breaking up) or demerging the company, distributing the proceeds to shareholders in either shares in the demerged company or in cash. British American Tobacco did this in giving shares in its Argos catalogue sales subsidiary to the existing shareholders and floating it on the market as a separate entity. It was a highly successful move.

HOW DOES SHAREHOLDER VALUE ANALYSIS REALLY WORK?

Beneath the veneer of jargon shareholder value is neither complex nor revolutionary. Cash accounting has been around for many years and has the advantage of not being distorted by arbitrary accounting policies.

The essence of shareholder value is the application of cash accounting to the future predicted performance of the business as determined by the strategy. Using cash flow data in the discounting cash flow process will produce net present values of individual operating units. The focus of management effort is moved away from *profitability* to *cash generation*. The way it works is to identify the main factors that drive shareholder value and quantify the effects of the business strategy on the future overall shareholder return.

Shareholder value is driven by a combination of factors:

- sales levels, growth and continuity
- profit margins
- return on invested capital
  - debt plus equity
  - risk adjusted return on investment
- cash flow from trading
- cash flow from managing assets.

This data is about future projections arising out of implementing the strategy of the business. Two cash flow figures are derived from evaluation:

- the total future returns in free cash flow terms generated by each of the individual business units expressed in present value terms over the timescale of the strategic plan
- the potential future value of the business again expressed in present value terms, at the end of the strategic plan.

The combination of the sum available for dividend payment and the potential value of the business is the shareholder value.

The evaluation of cash generation performance at a business unit level enables improved financial resource allocation by identifying which units are most likely to return the largest cash sums as a result of investment. In short, those units better at managing and generating cash are rewarded by future investment.

Summary

Shareholder value has several advantages over traditional methods of performance analysis:

- it avoids the temptation to manipulate profits by creative accounting techniques
- it brings a greater awareness of the importance of cash to operating managers
- it lines up the decision-making process for major investments in the business (capex), which are evaluated using DCF techniques with the reporting procedures that were historically profit-based
- it identifies clearly the parts of the business generating cash, which will be essential for future investment in the business, and helps with resource allocation decisions
- it attempts to quantify the strategic direction of the business and relate this to future shareholder return
- it supplies better quality data for communicating to investment professionals and as a result improves investor relations and corporate image.

10

ANALYSING AND PREDICTING COMPANY FAILURE

CHAPTER OBJECTIVES
- To attempt to answer the question – can it really be done?
- To examine the role that analysis of published accounts can play
- To provide a checklist of other factors which might help to predict failure

---

It seems appropriate for the last section of this book to look at the end in the life of a company. It is difficult to predict when the downfall will come. If a reliable mechanism could be designed then one of two situations would result:

- failure would never happen as corrective action of some kind would be taken to ensure it never did
- it would become a self-fulfilling prophecy as suppliers and bankers withdrew credit facilities and customers lost confidence.

Some attempts have been made to create such a mechanism. The main one was called, perhaps appropriately, 'Z-scoring'. This technique involved comprehensive credit scoring based on analysis of past financial statements. The theory has been tested on a sample of bankrupt and non-bankrupt companies and the results showed that it was valid – in around half the bankruptcy cases. As the great Lord Leverhulme, formerly Chairman of Lever Brothers (later to become part of Unilever), once said of his advertising spend, 'only half is useful but no one can tell me which half'. It is similar with Z-scoring.

The first section of this book looked at the past performance of a company in terms of doing a jigsaw puzzle. Some of the information that can be potentially helpful in predicting corporate failure is the same, except that we do not have all the pieces, are not sure what size they are, and are uncertain of their shapes.

WHAT ARE THE MOST LIKELY REASONS FOR GOING OUT OF BUSINESS?

The most common reason for going out of business is quite simply that the company runs out of cash at a critical time. The problem here is usually poor financial management, either short term or a failure to fund the permanent investment from long term sources resulting in working capital being squeezed to make up the shortfall. There are many reasons why a business may get into this position:

- inability to collect cash owed from debtors
- withdrawal of borrowing facilities
- speculation – defined as beyond risk management – using financial derivatives
- investment in fixed assets – using short term finance and failing to produce short term returns
- stock building – either voluntary or involuntary
- enforced payment of creditors – to maintain supplies and retain confidence
- failure to restrict non-productive costs to a level appropriate for the volume of business
- uninsured asset losses
- uneconomic pricing policies.

Every aspect of running a business has a cash flow implication. Effective business management monitors the causes and effects of events and decisions on a continuous basis. The following are essential guidelines:

- stick close to your customer – be ready for his *next* demand
- make friends with key suppliers both of services and materials – without them you will not be able to satisfy your customer

- monitor cash flow continuously. Cash flow through a business is like blood running through the veins of a body. When it is properly supplied and maintained it can produce its own supply – and even donate to others. Small amounts can be lost regularly without significant harm – a cut finger – but major losses – a severed artery – are going to require a transfusion. Even with this influx, unless the artery is repaired and the outflow stops, the transfusion will need repeating and ultimately supplies from the blood bank will be exhausted. Miracles are the only possibility at this stage, and relying on them is a risky strategy.

WHAT CAN READING THE REPORT AND ACCOUNTS TELL US?

Problems that can be identified from published accounts can be grouped into three categories: easily identifiable, more digging to do and no warning.

Easily identifiable

Event	*Implications*
• Huge increase in creditors (payables)	Inability to maintain previous payment patterns
• Huge increase in stocks (inventory)	Inability to sell product Change of stock valuation accounting policy Creative accounting?
• Reduction in cash:	
– free cash flow reduced	Problems at operating level – cost, volume or pricing
– lower closing figure (but still positive)	Not serious – but a trend to monitor
• Increase in borrowings:	Blood transfusion without arterial repair?
– short term	– could be a problem if at floating rates
– long term	– less of a problem with timescale and probably at fixed rates
• Reduction in investment for the future	Influenced by cash shortages rather than real business need
• Reduction in dividend payment	A worrying sign of a lack of confidence in the future

The relationship between the levels of:
• creditors
• sales
• margins
• debtors

can be revealing. In isolation each has a context, together they can indicate how the business is interacting with the market in the short term.

Illustration

Scenario				*Potential problem*
Sales stagnant	→ and	Debtors rising	→	Credit control
Debtors falling	→ and	Creditors rising	→	Cash flow
Sales falling	→ and	Stocks rising	→	Stock control
Stocks falling	→ and	Creditors rising	→	Cash flow

More digging to do – notes and policies

Study the accounting policies to identify any changes and read the notes to see the quantified effect of them.

Illustration

- **Capitalisation Policies.** These attempt to take cost out of the profit and loss statement and on to the assets in the balance sheet (see Queens Moat Houses case). A typical example would be to include the interest cost on money borrowed for a building as part of the final asset value or to include the cost of work done by permanently employed staff as adding to the asset value rather than as an expense. The impact of this kind of policy is to distort profit but increase capital expenditure, viewed positively as investment for the future. In the cash flow statement it would move some operating costs down to capex.
- **Frequent revaluation of assets.** In an attempt to strengthen the balance sheet frequent *upward* revaluations can be carried out. It was much easier to do this under high inflationary conditions. The outlook for the future probably makes this one difficult now, but in the past it was a good game.

No warning

The accounts do not reveal everything. Developments in financial reporting are making them more meaningful but the wider environment will critically affect the survival and prosperity of the company. Many clues to potential liquidity problems are buried within totalled numbers, even after seeing more detailed analyses in the notes, for example reduced spending on advertising and marketing. Another sign would be the use of debt factoring or invoice discounting.

Published accounts are inevitably historic. Some problems are only allowed to emerge when it is time for the auditors to 'sign off' the accounts – and they frequently force the issue. Stock Exchange regulations force announcements to be made and the enforcement of these rules is getting tougher (see London International Group case). Directors commit a criminal offence by 'trading whilst insolvent', defined as 'incurring liabilities without the prospect of being able to meet them'. It is difficult, however, to prove this offence in law and few cases exist. Sadly, many of these events are only revealed too late to save the company in anything like its previous state.

WHAT OTHER INFORMATION MIGHT HELP?

Back to the jigsaw puzzle again. There are some helpful items – many innocent in isolation – which together will begin to provide a picture of looming problems.

Checklist of predictive events – outside the numbers

- Non-standard accounting policies and practices compared with competitors and the industry.
- Rapid expansion { sales volumes, headcount, capital employed.
- Failure to produce financial reports and accounts on time.
- Combined Chief Executive and Chairman role, particularly when compounded by a large personal shareholding.
- Dominant and flamboyant personalities at the top of the company.
- Frequency of boardroom resignations.
- Directors' share transactions (reported in Saturday's *Financial*

Times for UK listed companies), particularly just before the 'closed' period (seven weeks before results announcements).
- Moving from asset purchase to leasing.
- Highly acquisitive.
- Unexplained inter-company transactions within a group.
- Auditor quality. There is evidence that not having a 'Big-6' firm increases risk (see Queens Moat Houses case).

Summary

Many companies do survive even though they display several of the predictive events. Perhaps this is through luck or management. Both come in two varieties – good and bad. It is difficult to control the first so rely upon the second to exploit good luck and minimise the effect of the bad luck.

HAPPY FINANCIAL MANAGEMENT

11

CASE STUDIES

CLARKE FOODS PLC

The Clarke Foods case brings together many aspects of financial management although it had only a short life.

Key case points

- Acquisition valuation
- The difference between running a large company and a small one
- Ownership structures
- Pitfalls in the long term financing of a company
- Pitfalls in the short term financing of a company
- Dividend policy

Background

In 1991 Clarke Foods was Britain's second largest ice cream manufacturer with 13 per cent of the UK's £800m market. It was quoted on the USM and was run by Henry D. Clarke Jr who made the Klondike bar into the US's best selling novelty ice cream product. The company started its life in 1991 when it acquired the ice cream businesses owned by Hillsdown Holdings in a share swap for a stake in Henry D. Clarke Jr's private investment company Yelverton Investments. The acquisition consisted of some neglected manufacturing facilities and some down-market brands, the best known of which was Fiesta.

The development of the company

Clarke immediately embarked on a £12m capital investment programme to install high technology manufacturing equipment to enable
a greater variety of high-quality products to be produced in substantial
volumes.

It made commercial sense to find an established product range to
utilise this capacity. In January 1992, Clarke announced the purchase
from Allied Lyons for £12m of the Lyons Maid brand name, including
the Zoom rocket bar and Mivvi lolly. A major additional asset was the
distribution network of 20,000 accounts. Additionally, Clarke took responsibility for creditor payments, raising the total consideration to
£13.3m. Strategically, the actions looked correct and were supported
by the shareholders in a successful 2 for 3 rights issue which raised
£6.8m cash, largely to pay for the Lyons Maid acquisition. The Clarke
family took up most of their rights with their stake marginally diluting
from 33 per cent to 27 per cent. Hillsdown Holdings took up its rights
to maintain their holding at 17 per cent. Other institutional shareholders largely made up the balance of ownership and were happy with
the issue.

Although soundly financed by committed shareholders, the strategy
looked ambitious:

- to turn around a manufacturing business
- to commission state of the art facilities
- to revive a well-known but long-neglected brand name.

Henry Clarke certainly cannot be accused of having lacked courage.
He added to all these plans the launch of the modestly titled Clarke Bar,
a premium take-home product, emblazoned with his photograph as a 7-
year-old on the packaging. He even backed his judgement by mounting
a million-pound advertising campaign to promote it, in addition to the
£5m budgeted for the existing planned range of products.

The situation in 1992

The early part of 1992 exposed the optimism of the strategy as the UK
continued to suffer the longest recession in consumer spending since
the 1930s. Although much thought analysis and resources are put into

formulating a business plan there will always be uncertainty and uncontrollable risks. Ice cream making is still a seasonal industry despite the efforts of the marketing and advertising people to encourage all-year-round consumption. An overriding factor, which Henry may not have fully appreciated from his Florida home, is the UK weather.

Setbacks in commissioning the equipment meant that instead of producing ice cream from February 1992, the factories were not operational until July. August is the peak sales month in the UK – at least in most years – but not in 1992, when rainfall was the heaviest for half a century. In a similar way to how Allied Lyons believed the dollar could not continue rising in early 1991 (see Allied Lyons case). Henry thought the rain could not continue falling in August, so he put the factories on round the clock production. The level of output was high, fixed costs were being recovered over large volumes, and unit costs were falling. When overdue deliveries were made the profits would follow.

That was the theory. The retailers saw it differently, not wanting to carry high stocks late in the season. Orders dried up and the delivery backlog evaporated. Ice cream can be stored, but there are two costs involved: capital expenditure on freezing facilities and the electricity cost of running them for 24 hours a day. Both of these costs hit the cash and to some extent the profitability.

The long term sources of finance to the business can ensure the business survives short term operational problems. No negative points in this case, as ownership was well structured. It would have been too early – after only six months – to go for another rights issue. It may also have been difficult for the Clarke family to find the cash to enable them to maintain their ownership percentage, and dilution below 25 per cent would have taken away their 'blocking' holding. The announcement of a rights issue would also have necessitated a profits warning, which could not have been optimistic.

Long term borrowings were £6m – £3m for plant expenditure and the balance for general business needs. In financial management terms a larger loan for the equipment would have been desirable, although only £6m actual cash was paid to Alfa Laval, the supplier of the £12m worth of equipment. A weakness could be the value of collateral provided for the bank debt. It is always desirable to provide the minimum to cover the loan, thus allowing further potential borrowing. Unfortunately, if the bank took a hard view of resale asset values rather than costs this may be the maximum it was prepared to advance.

Short term borrowing facilities appeared to be both substantial and appropriate in widening the variety of potential sources. The company had in place an invoice discounting facility to fund working capital. This is appropriate if the majority of the working capital investment is receivables, because finance only becomes available when invoices are raised. Where products go into inventory rather than being sold, no finance is provided. As the latter was the situation in this case, Clarke had acute cash flow problems despite having an £8m facility and only using £2.5m of it. The offer from Lombard Invoice Discounting to advance 60 per cent rather than 55 per cent of invoice values did not help the situation at all as there were no invoiced sales being made as September approached. Retailers were fully stocked after poor August sales. It is sad if a finance provider does not understand the business and position of a company. A failure to keep providers fully informed is essential if workable solutions are to be achieved.

The crisis

The critical cash shortage became dramatically public on 14 September when the company announced that the interim dividend of 0.75p per share announced on 3 August would not be paid. The shares fell from 64p to 21p. Creditors and suppliers were threatening action and the company 'opened talks' with its bankers. Critical elements in determining dividend policy are ensuring there is the cash to pay it and also assessing the impact of taking cash permanently out of the business.

Henry Clarke himself feels a flaw in the financial structure was the low equity. In his words, 'You can't slug it out with Unilever with only £17m net worth. We probably needed to raise another £8m but it would have been better with £15m.' If this is correct, any entry to a market where there is a large multi-national is doomed. Perhaps just being less ambitious on time scale and on the number of objectives is an alternative answer.

The conclusion to the story is that Clarke went into administrative receivership on 13 October. There were debts of around £25m, including £3.4m to Allied Lyons, £6m to Natwest Bank and £6m to Alfa Laval. Hillsdown Holdings had to take £7.6m provision against loss of its equity investment. The main assets and business were acquired by Nestlé in December 1992 for £40.5m, beating off a strong challenge by Mars.

TRAFALGAR HOUSE PLC

An early case illustration of how the changing world of UK financial reporting is affecting the presentation of company financial information. Trafalgar House is a well–established company with considerable interests in property and related activities.

Key case points

- Accounting policies
- The impact of new Financial Reporting Standards
- The influence of the Financial Reporting Review Panel
- The difference between ownership and control
- The wider implications of adverse publicity

Background

Trafalgar House plc is a London-based international group with interests in engineering, construction, commercial and residential property together with a small fleet of luxury cruise ships, including the Queen Elizabeth II, and three London hotels, the largest of which is the Ritz. It became a listed company in 1963 under the leadership of Sir Nigel Broackes who remained Chairman until late 1992.

The City only loves companies run by entrepreneurial chief executives while they are successful. It is often only too eager to disown companies which have failed to 'play by the rules'. Over-optimistic profit forecasts and doubtful accounting policies are early signs of disillusionment. Trafalgar had also a record of ill-timed and expensive acquisitions. In July 1991 it paid £114m for Davy Engineering. Since then it has had to inject more than £100m for additional working capital. It surely has to be considered whether the due diligence process should have pointed to some of these potential problems. The result of this was to raise gearing to high levels, adding to the group's vulnerability.

The intervention from the Far East

Jardine Matheson, the Hong Kong trading conglomerate, surprised the financial community on 1 October 1991 by mounting a dawn raid to acquire 14.9 per cent of the company through its subsidiary, Hong Kong Land. It announced its intention to build the stake up to 29.9 per cent which is the maximum holding without mounting a full takeover bid under the London Stock Exchange's City Takeover Code.

Jardine knows the business well. It has been in partnership in Hong Kong as Gammon Construction for some years. Was it a case of a wealthy experienced predator identifying an attractive opportunity? The evidence points both ways. Trafalgar in early October 1991 was highly geared and operating in a number of diverse unfashionable businesses. Shipbuilders, engineering and construction had all been badly hit by worldwide recession and very harsh competition. Margins had been decimated. Cunard looked like a relic of the past, as did the Ritz hotel – poor occupancy levels were driving profits through the floor. On the positive side, many of the core businesses were good cash generators requiring minimal long term investment. If economies start to expand again construction is often an early beneficiary. The share price had dropped by two-thirds in five months – perhaps the time and the price were right.

The 1991 reports and accounts

A major reason for the weakness of the company was the considerable adverse publicity generated by the accounting policies adopted in the 1991 accounts. The principal one causing concern was the reclassification of development properties as fixed assets rather than current assets. As inventory they would have been valued according to the normal accounting convention of 'cost or market value whichever is the lower' and any write-down would have been taken through the profit statement. Trafalgar was reluctant to do this as the size of the write-off was £102.7m, reducing the pre-stated profit of £122.4m to just £19.7m. By changing the policy the write-down applied to a change in value of a fixed asset which could be 'taken through reserves', i.e. just deducted from a revaluation surplus in the balance sheet, leaving the profit statement unaffected.

This 'interesting' treatment caught the attention of the UK's new regime of standard setters. Firstly, the Finance Reporting Review Panel (FRRP) launched an investigation into the specific circumstances. This was reported on the front page of the *Financial Times*, underlying the belief that publicity would be the major weapon of the FRRP. The effect on the share price was devastating and some of the later board-room changes originated from this time. Despite early strong objections, Trafalgar agreed to restate 1991 profits. When other accounting policies were adjusted the revised figure became a loss of £38.5m.

The offer to acquire a further 15 per cent of shares at 85p by a tendering process was perhaps optimistic on Jardine's part. Shareholders could have been forgiven for thinking a takeover offer was on the way. The Far Eastern way of doing things is more subtle but highly effective. It was no surprise that the tender offer failed with only another 1 per cent of shares acquired. Boardroom changes were, however, on the way, both the Chairman and the Chief Executive stepping down and a Hong Kong Land representative, Rodney Leach, joined the board. Further representation was being sought. There were also signs less than a month after the failure of the tender offer that some shareholders could be reconsidering. Jardine secured an option to buy 36 million shares at 85p on 3 February 1993, taking its stake to 20.07 per cent. There could have been further obligations to buy but they were limited to 29.9 per cent.

The 1992 situation

Trafalgar reported a further loss of £30.3m for its year ending 30 September 1992 after exceptional profit write-downs of £138m. Concern was expressed by Trafalgar over the 'significant amount of control' exercised by Jardine with only a minority holding. Both the Stock Exchange and the takeover panel described the arrangement as 'right and proper'.

By mid-1993, Jardine had four representatives on the board including the Chairman, Finance Director and two non-executives. Its holding had been taken up to 25 per cent, almost mirroring the picture at Kwik-Save plc, the highly successful UK discount supermarket group, where Dairy Farm, the food retailing arm of Jardine, holds 29.9 per cent of the shares. The last two Kwik-Save chief executives formerly worked for Dairy Farm companies. Jardine may have hit on a controversial method of influencing and controlling companies, but if it can deliver results like Kwik-Save with fast organic growth rates, improving margins and zero borrowings the protests are likely to be muted

QUEENS MOAT HOUSES PLC

Queens Moat Houses was a rapidly expanding hotel group with interests in the UK and Continental Europe. It had grown by both acquisition and organic growth financed by both share issues and debt.

Key case points

- Creative accounting policies
- Funding decisions
- General financial management of a public listed company
- Corporate failure

Background

Queens Moat Houses had been built up by an entrepreneurial boss, John Bairstow, who started by opening up part of his own house in Essex as an hotel in the 1940s. At its height the company had 103 hotels in the UK, mainly in provincial locations, and 86 hotels (including franchised ones) in Continental Europe. They were operated under the brand names of Moat Houses, Queens Hotels and Classic Hotels. Some retained an individual identity, others in Continental Europe were franchised under the Holiday Inn, Ramada and Ibis names.

The situation in 1991

The picture revealed in the accounts for the year ended 31 December 1991 still looked apparently healthy. Turnover had risen in the year from £484.5m to £543.3m, pre-tax profits had fallen only modestly from £94.1m to £90.4m, and net assets had grown from £1,168.9m to £1,297.9m. Cash had increased from £76.4m to £381.5m. Dividend increases of 10 per cent had been recommended 'reflecting the board's confidence in the future'. The accounts had been signed without qualification by the auditor, Bird Luckin, on 30 April 1992.

The accounting policies

Careful reading of the report revealed some interesting accounting policies. Under 'Profit before rent and interest' it states that this figure reflects the results achieved in the normal course of business. Part of this figure is income from the controversial management incentive scheme, which applied to 62 of the 103 hotels in the UK and 15 out of the 37 European hotels. The scheme, which had operated since 1975, gave each self-employed manager an unlimited earnings potential in return for agreeing to a guaranteed minimum cash payment to Queens Moat. The amount was normally 25–30 per cent of the budgeted annual turnover. It was the manager's responsibility to control operating costs and worry about occupancy levels.

The policy did flatter profits by including the income for the *following* year as income for *this* year. In buoyant, inflationary times when incomes were rising this was not a problem. It also gave a one-off boost to profits when another hotel was added to the scheme. For example, if an hotel entered the scheme in 1989/90 the payment would be based on the budget for 1990/91, treated as 1989/90 income and cash not paid until 1990/91.

The impact of the incentive scheme on profit was significant. The introduction of the same accounting policy to the German hotels would have increased profits by £20m in 1992. Also not included in the profit statement was 'expenditure incurred in the creation and marketing of new projects'. This was capitalised and included such items as interest, pre-opening marketing expenses, professional fees and maintenance wages. Another useful policy was to include profits and losses on disposal of fixed assets calculated as the difference between sale proceeds and depreciated historic cost, although they were included in the balance sheet at valuation making the asset value as high as possible. The policy on depreciation of fixed assets helped to increase the profit. Fixtures, fittings, plant and equipment were not depreciated, and certain repairs and maintenance expenditures were capitalised.

Financing the expansion

If the lenders and financial markets noticed these policies it certainly did not affect the share price significantly or the ability of the company to raise cash (see Table 11.1). During 1991 a successful rights issue raised £183m and a 10.25 per cent debenture stock raised £88m for 30 years at a fixed rate.

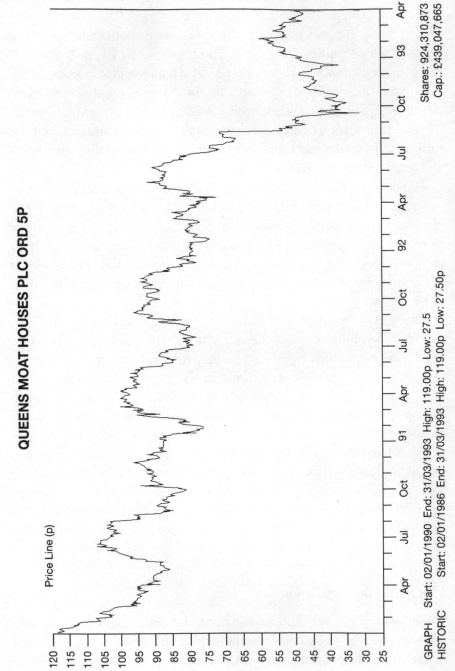

QUEENS MOAT HOUSES PLC ORD 5P

Price Line (p)

GRAPH   Start: 02/01/1990 End: 31/03/1993 High: 119.00p Low: 27.5
HISTORIC   Start: 02/01/1986 End: 31/03/1993 High: 119.00p Low: 27.50p

Shares: 924,310,873
Cap.: £439,047,665

Figure 11.1

Table 11.1   Changes in long term debt and fixed asset values

Long term debt (£m)	1986	1987	1988	1989	1990	1991	1992	1993
Debt	107	297	411	605	760	1,121	1,345	1,434
Fixed asset values	355	688	1,054	1,467	1,970	2,145	892	927

More interesting revelations

A number of other warning signs were present in the accounts. The auditor, Bird Luckin, is not well known for being associated with large company audits. The former senior partner was, at the end of 1991, a non-executive director of Queens Moat and chairman of two key non-executive committees – Audit and remuneration. Transactions between directors and Queens Moat occurred, mainly involving the acquisition of subsidiaries in which directors had shareholdings. An example was the acquisition of Chester International Hotel plc in which six directors of Queens Moat had holdings. Chester International Hotel plc was valued on 30 April 1992 at £9.5m and had made a loss of £40,000 after interest and tax during 1991. The directors' report clearly states that none of the six directors had taken part in the decision of the board regarding the terms of the offer.

The start of major problems

The often quoted saying 'Profit is a concept, cash is a fact' can be well applied here. Despite an apparently healthy cash figure at the end of 1991 and a statement in the accounts that the board has taken 'substantial and prudent measures to maintain financial strength and flexibility', the situation had deteriorated to the point that the then Chairman issued a statement on 31 March 1993 that the group's 1992 results were likely to fall seriously short of expectations and that the preference dividend due on 1 April 1993 could not be paid. The group's banks called in Grant Thornton to investigate the financial position. As a result the accounting policies were reviewed and Jones Lang Wootton were appointed to value the Group's properties.

The financial review resulted in a combined annual report and accounts for 1992 being prepared with an interim report for the first half of 1993 on 29 October 1993. This document, containing a restatement of the 1992 accounts, makes interesting reading. Key figures are:

	Original	*Restated*
Turnover	£543.3m	£314.7m
Pre-tax profits	£90.1m	£56.3m (loss)
Net assets	£1,297.9m	£1,192.6m
Cash (a reliable fact)		unchanged

The main reasons for these considerable changes can be analysed thus:

	Effect on:	
	Profit (£m)	*Assets* (£m)
Change in treatment of incentive fees (now only applied to the accounting period being reported)	(13.5)	(48.6)
Sales and leaseback transactions (now treated as finance leases and included as assets, recognising the future liability that will become outstanding)	(18.3)	(41.2)
Depreciation and repairs and maintenance (fixtures, fittings, plant equipment repairs and maintenance expenditure now being expensed)	(50.9)	(2.5)
Capitalised expenses (items such as interest, pre-opening marketing expenses and professional expenses now being expensed)	(21.9)	(21.9)

	Profit (£m)	Assets (£m)
Specific acquisition (a fee received previously treated as turnover rather than lowering the cost of an acquisition)	(10.3)	(–)
Profit on disposal of fixed assets (now calculated as the difference between sale proceeds and balance sheet value)	(24.2)	(–)

The valuation controversy

Although the restated figures for 1991 showed major differences, the 1992 report had to bear the impact of the reduction in property values which resulted from the independent valuation commissioned at the start of the financial review. At 31 December 1991, Weatherall Green and Smith (WGS) had valued the group's properties at £2bn and that figure had been incorporated in the audited balance sheet. Weatherall Green and Smith presented a draft valuation for 31 December 1993 to the previous board and a draft valuation at 31 March 1993 to the group's bankers in May 1993. Both of these valuations were considerably lower than the December 1991 valuation.

The Jones Lang Wootton valuation for 31 December 1992 was materially different to both the December 1991 figure and the May figure. It was £861m, a difference of £1,139m. The debates about valuation policy and method are set to continue for some time.

The results for 1992

The 1992 results show that the group incurred losses before taxation of over £1bn (£1,045.5m). Exceptional losses accounted for £939m of this, including £803.9m that reflected the Jones Lang Wootton property revaluation. This has led to the balance sheet showing net liabilities of £388.9m against net borrowings of £1,165.9m. All the previous executive directors resigned and have made various claims against the company. The report notes tersely that 'all these claims are being strongly resisted' and 'the company may have rights of action against previous directors or advisers'. On the topic of financial restructuring, the Chairman states, 'Your board believes that the level of cash flow generated from the group's operations will be insufficient for the foreseeable future to service the current level of the group's indebtedness on the basis of the financing arrangements which existed as at 31 March 1993. A financial restructuring is essential for the group, including inevitably a debt for equity swap which will dilute shareholders' interests'.

Restructuring carries with it some heavy costs. The charges, including facilities fees, will be at least £42m. Delays in reaching agreement with 74 lenders, who have been presented with a debt-for-equity swap, has led to increased costs. The new board has certainly evaluated the situation quickly and started on the inevitable long and arduous road from a very difficult position.

LONDON WEEKEND TELEVISION PLC

Key case points

- Innovative financing
- Financially incentivising management
- Financial response to changing industry structure
- Enhancing shareholder value
- Acquisition valuation
- Capital expenditure decision-making

Background

A decade ago the British television industry was stable and protected. The two national State broadcasting channels (BBC 1 and BBC 2) were financed via a licence fee payable by all television viewers. Its value was set by the Government and broadly increased at the rate of retail price inflation. The two regional commercial channels were financed mainly from air-time advertising sales, and the Government taxed commercial television in two ways: a specific industry levy and normal corporation tax.

In 1986 a Government report into the future of broadcasting proposed far reaching changes. The author of the report, Sir Alan Peacock, described the system as a 'comfortable duopoly'. Although the only immediate effect of the report was related to the means of determining the licence fee for the next several years, another of its key recommendations was to have profound implications for the industry. Its recommendation that each network had to source 25 per cent of its programming from independent producers was to change the structure and balance of the broadcasting and production business.

Further impetus for change came in the Broadcasting Act of 1990, which introduced an auction process for the main commercial channel, to be renamed Channel 3. A new statutory body, the Independent Television Commission (ITC), was set up to supervise the auction process and to award new regional broadcasting franchises to commence on 1 January 1993. The Government hoped to increase the tax revenue from the broadcasting industry by introducing greater commercial reality. Estimates from brokers in 1992 forecast an increase in tax take of £40m.

The existing structure divided the country into regions and gave each company the exclusive right to broadcast programmes and sell advertising air time, within strictly controlled limits, in its own region. Breakfast television was treated as national with a single broadcaster, and the London region had a weekday and weekend broadcaster.

The auction process

The first stage of the process required all applicants to pass a quality threshold. Only those applicants satisfying this criterion were able to submit their business plan and the amount of their annual bid payment. This last element was to be in a sealed bid, thus maximising, at least in theory, the tax take. There was a minimum bid of £1,000. For the potential bidders the auction bid became an enormous capital investment project. For existing licence holders it was also their existing business – failure to regain the licence meant closure of their operation.

London Weekend Television

London Weekend Television (LWT) was the holder of the licence to broadcast television programmes throughout London from 5.15pm on Friday to the close of transmission on Sunday. The board recognised in 1988 the possibility that its business could disappear at the end of 1992. It was determined to regain the licence but had an alternative plan in reserve. The contingency involved forming separate companies for broadcasting, programme making, advertising sales, facilities hire and property management – allowing them to continue as operating businesses even without a broadcasting licence.

A small core team working closely with advisers defined an essential series of pre-conditions to enable the company to focus on regaining the licence. These pre-conditions were:

- to enhance shareholder value and reduce risk
- to inhibit takeover
- to introduce financial discipline to the business
- to make cost control a prime objective
- to lock in key personnel.

A scheme was devised to include a refinancing package to meet these objectives. The main elements were:

- a special dividend utilising all the cash and exhausting the borrowing potential of the business
- a loan note promising repayment in 1993 to be met either from selling off assets or companies if the bid was unsuccessful, or from operating cash flow if the licence were regained
- the issue of a preferred share, paying a fixed dividend, exchangeable for an ordinary share in late 1993.

The introduction of a share scheme enabled the 40 (increased progressively to 54) key executives to buy 'management shares' at the current market rate (83p), payable in cash. The cost to the management was £3m, for which they got 3 per cent of the company. The real incentive was the 'ratchet' characteristic of these management shares. In short, if the LWT quoted share price rose then the management would be issued with extra free shares. In this way the management could eventually own 15 per cent of the company; but there were conditions. For the full ratchet to take effect (four free shares for each one held) the quoted price would have to rise to £2.78 and stay there for 20 days in the autumn of 1993. It is very unlikely this figure would have been achieved without regaining the licence.

The total value of the refinancing package, together with the quoted preferred share, corresponded broadly with the previous quoted ordinary share value. The scheme was approved by 82 per cent of shareholders. The pre-conditions had all been met in the following ways:

Enhancing shareholder value and reducing risk	– Immediate distribution of special dividend – Future distribution planned – Regular fixed dividend (yield 5 per cent) – Up-side potential retained by conversion to ordinary share
Inhibit takeover	– Restricted rights of preferred share
Financial discipline	– Introduced by replacing interest receivable of £6.5m with interest payable of virtually the same amount arising out of borrowings, secured on the buildings, made to pay the special dividend
Cost control	– Made vital to maintain interest payments and stay within covenants
Lock in key personnel	– Achieved by the incentive share scheme for key executives

For the company the days of being cash rich were over. Tight covenants relating to all aspects of performance were in place. Capital expenditure was restricted and cost control was vital to keep within cash limits. There was now a single clear focus for the business.

The recognition that people were the most important element in the business was a crucial factor. The share scheme locked in and motivated key executives for effectively five years. Uniquely, the interests of shareholders and management were fused – both were to benefit hugely if the bid was successful. Cleverly, this prevented a huge lump sum bid. Some other bidders, notably the Yorkshire regional holder, took a different route. Their incentive was a 'success' fee to key executives payable simply for winning. In basic terms, the surest way to win was to bid the highest, using shareholders' money which potentially could have been dividends. Cost reduction to meet dividend payments would have to be carefully handled as it was difficult to compromise on programme quality and still be certain of passing this threshold, particularly for an existing broadcaster.

The brilliance of the scheme is further evident from the additional control aspects. Firstly, the executives could not sell any shares until August 1993 – following the important transition year (1992) and well into the first year of the new licence. Thus a rapid price movement after the announcement of the auction results on 16 October 1991 had to be followed for 22 months by a level of performance capable of moving the share price upwards to make the reward substantial. The fact that the ratchet could not be triggered before 31 August 1993 meant the real 'jackpot' of extra shares would only become available if the share price was beyond £2.78 on that day and had met the 20-day measure as well. Even then executives had to submit to the board a request to sell a number of shares and agree to sell no more for a further year. There was to be, in the words of an insider, 'an orderly disposal'. Thus the fortunes of the key executives were tied to long term business performance, but 85 per cent of the improvement would go to existing shareholders – surely a true enhancement of 'shareholder value'.

Before these riches could be realised the management had a series of difficult tasks: to pass the quality threshold, to beat the competition and win the licence with an annual payment that would enable a profitable future to be predicted and reflected in the share price. Essentially it was a capital expenditure decision – make a long term investment now and hope for returns in the future – but with an important difference. Normally, when capital expenditure decisions are made, the amount of initial investment is known with future returns being uncertain. In this case the original (and annual) investment had to be predicted as well as the future returns. Either way there was a problem: putting in a low figure might not win, submitting a high figure would raise questions about financial viability over the 10-year period, potentially compromising programme quality and limiting the scope for dividend payment.

The auction results

The auction produced some astounding results (see Table 11.1). London Weekend Television was successful with a bid of £7.58m, the lowest of the nine 'large' regions. As in traditional fairy stories there was a happy ending – or perhaps two. The share price rose beyond the £2.78 threshold, and LWT took a 14.9 per cent stake in a weaker regional broadcaster, Yorkshire, which had itself merged with Tyne Tees. With the share price at £3.75 things were looking good both for the company and the executives, although one uncertainty remained. The Government had imposed a moratorium on takeover bids for the nine largest broadcasting licence holders under the 1990 Broadcasting Act, which had divided companies into 'large' (nine regions) and 'small' (six regions). Cross-holdings were allowed but restrictions applied. There was a strong prospect that some liberalisation of the rules would be allowed which could have far reaching implications on the structure of the industry.

Table 11.1 The bidders

Region	Company	Bid	Quality threshold
Breakfast TV	SUNRISE	£34.61m	✓
	TV-am	£14.13m	✓
	Daybreak	£33.30m	✓
London weekday	CARLTON TV	£43.17m	✓
	Thames	£32.70m	✓
	CPV-TV	£45.32m	✗
London weekend	LONDON WEEKEND	£7.58m	✓
	London Independent Broadcasting	£35.41m	✗
Midlands	CENTRAL	£2,000	✓
North West	GRANADA	£9.00m	✓
	North West TV	£35.30m	✗
Yorkshire	YORKSHIRE TV	£37.70m	✓
	White Rose TV	£17.40m	✓
	Viking TV	£30.12m	✗
South and South East	MERIDIAN BROADCASTING	£36.52m	✓
	TVS	£59.76m	✓
	Carlton TV	£18.08m	✓
	CPV-TV	£22.11m	✗
Wales and West	HTV	£20.53m	✓
	Merlin	£19.36m	✗
	Chanel 3 Wales & West	£18.29m	✗
	C3W	£17.76m	✓
East	ANGLIA	£17.80m	✓
	Three East	£14.08m	✓
	CPV-TV	£10.13m	✗
North East	TYNE TEES	£15.06m	✓
	North East TV	£5.01m	✓
Central Scotland	SCOTTISH TV	£2,000	✓
South West	WEST COUNTRY TV	£7.82m	✓
	TSW	£16.12m	✓
	Telewest	£7.27m	✗
Northern Ireland	ULSTER	£1.03m	✓
	Lagan TV	£2.71m	✗
	TVNi	£3.10m	✓
North of Scotland	GRAMPIAN	£0.72m	✓
	C3 Caledonia	£1.13m	✗
	North of Scotland TV	£2.71m	✗
Borders	BORDER TV	£52,000	✓
Channel Islands	CHANNEL TV	£1,000	✓
	C3	£102,000	✓

Successful bidders

A dramatic event on 29 June 1993 changed the value of LWT. Granada acquired a 14.9 per cent holding from three institutional holders at what seemed like the premium share price of 500p per share. In August, 1993 with the share price hovering at this level, the biggest employee payout in British corporate history took place when £70 million of shares were distributed to 54 executives. Sixteen became millionaires overnight and another nine had shareholdings worth in excess of £900,000. Approximately one-third of their shares were sold, mainly to repay loans originally taken to finance share purchase, leaving the management holding at 10 per cent.

The easing of ownership restrictions and its impact on LWT

In late November the Government eased the restrictions rather unexpectedly, opening the way for one company to own two regional licences, whether large or small. The route for Granada was open and on 3 December a full bid was made. The Granada shareholding stood at 17.5 per cent and it hoped for an agreed bid.

The final chapter

The offer was not viewed as generous in the heady atmosphere of the time, valuing the shares at 580.5p with a cash alternative of 528p. The cash alternative was mandatory under the City takeover code as Granada had bought shares for cash within the past 12 months. Normally, bidders have to offer a premium to gain acceptance, typically 30 per cent over the market price. The Granada bid was in fact a discount of just 0.8 per cent. The value of the company had grown dramatically since the refinancing scheme. In 1989 the value was £73m, while in 1993 it had become £481m, an increase of 660 per cent.

The offer was rejected by the LWT board. All acquisitors prefer agreed bids and Granada always hoped for an endorsement. This it never achieved, but it was ultimately successful with a revised offer of 13 new Granada shares and 100p in cash for every 10 LWT shares. The cash alternative was increased to 686p, an increase of 30 per cent from the original offer. This valued the company at £760m.

A key player in deciding the fate of the company was Mercury Asset Management, a fund associated with the merchant bank S. G. Warburg.

It held 14.2 per cent of LWT shares and 16.4 per cent of Granada shares. In such a powerful position, the smaller institutions waited to see what action Mercury would take. In the end it took the unusual step of announcing its decision to sell before the closing date, thus sealing the fate of the bid. LWT ceased to be a quoted company but its place in UK corporate history is assured.

LONDON INTERNATIONAL GROUP (FORMERLY LONDON RUBBER CO)

London International Group is a UK public listed company. Its shares are also quoted through ADRs on the NASDAQ system in the US. The operating divisions of the company manufacture and market high-quality branded goods and services. At its peak it operated in over 120 countries, had an annual turnover of £400m and employed more than 10,000 people.

Key case points

- Corporate collapse
- Brand valuation
- Rights issues
- Acquisition/diversification strategy
- Low interest convertible finance

Background

London International Group is a health products and toiletries company which is the world leader in branded condoms under the DUREX brand. Other brand names used by the company include Marigold rubber gloves, Woodward's gripe water, Wrights coal tar soap, Eucryl tooth powder and Buttercup cough medicine.

In the early 1980s it embarked on an ambitious diversification programme in an attempt to compensate for the expected long term decline in the condom business. In 1982 LIG's share of the condom market in the UK was 95 per cent, and internationally 35 per cent. The main diversification was into photoprocessing, thought to be a growth business with high margins produced by advances in technology and growing consumer spending. Investment on acquisitions in this area, starting in 1982, reached £70m. The results up to 1991 looked promising. Financial highlights gave no warning signals in the annual report issued in June 1992 (see Table 11.2).

Table 11.2

	Pre-tax profits (£m)	Earnings per share (pence)	Dividends per share (pence)
1982	9.0	7.49	2.42
1983	11.6	7.40	2.86
1984	13.5	8.22	3.39
1985	16.5	8.27	3.90
1986	21.8	10.74	4.60
1987	25.2	12.81	5.40
1988	27.1	14.92	6.30
1989	28.0	14.69	7.25
1990	34.2	17.64	8.35
1991	39.3	20.17	9.25

The successful rights issue

In January 1991 the company had been successful in raising £62m in a rights issue on the basis of one new share for every four held. This was needed to provide the sum of £50m before March 1992 when convertible bond holders could have requested payment. The convertible bonds were issued in 1987 at an interest rate of 4.5 per cent, and can be converted into ordinary shares at a price of £4.30 at any time up to March 2002. As the Chairman said in the 1991 report, 'In the current market it is likely that the bonds will be redeemed on the first redemption date'. The share price in June 1991 was £2.25. The benefit to the company had been the ability to borrow money at 4.5 per cent at a time when market rates would have been between 8 per cent and 14 per cent.

The 1990 results

The balance sheet did contain £42m of intangible assets (brands and patents) compared with fixed assets of £1,091m, but among them is DUREX, which has achieved the ultimate status for a brand of being incorporated as a generic word in the language, alongside such names as Hoover and Biro. The accounting policies stated that these assets were not depreciated. Acquisitions were continuing in that year, although only on a small scale of £8.2m. Interestingly, £7.6m of this was for 'goodwill', which under the accounting policy was taken out of retained profits – 'taking through reserves' – rather than through the profit and loss account.

The 1991 results

Once again, the company was able to report another year of progress, the twelfth consecutive year of increased turnover and profit. The highlights for 1992 are compared:

	Pre-tax profits	Earnings per share	Dividends per share
1991	£39.3m	20.17 pence	9.25 pence
1992	£39.4m	16.68 pence	9.45 pence

It perhaps looks more of a struggle here, and the report did not show a graphic on earnings per share as it had done the previous year.

The 1992 results

It was 1993 that saw the end of the unbroken run:

	Pre-tax profits	Earnings per share	Dividends per share
1993	£32.5m	13.02 pence	9.45 pence

While the core business – now redesignated as thin film technology – continued to perform well, the photoprocessing division was 'experiencing difficulties'. Although the company stressed that the investment had made it the lowest cost producer in the UK in this business, it did not emphasise that volume is the key to profit in this type of business.

The recession was affecting volumes and over-capacity in the industry was leading to 'significant price pressure'. The actions being taken were to 'take cost out' and the Chairman stated that the business was now managed on a 'broadly cash-neutral basis'. The ultimate solution to the problem was the success in winning the contract to process the films for Supasnaps, which has over 350 outlets in the UK. The gaining of a large order does not always lead to profitability – if the contract were secured at the expense of margins or unrealistic promises of service.

The Stock Exchange censure

It is normal to brief institutions and analysts regularly about the general trading situation of a company. It is in the interests of the company to ensure that the analysts' forecasts and the actual results are similar as shocks are bad for share prices. Any such shocks illustrate a lack of control and lower the level of confidence in the management of the business.

The company briefed 13 analysts and four institutions separately, indicating that the annual results would be below expectations. The Stock Exchange issued a public censure – its first ever – for revealing important information to a selected group rather than to the market generally. Under Exchange rules any information which might have an impact on the share price should be made through the official Company Announcements Office of the Stock Exchange. The impact in the future is likely to be that this channel will be used more frequently.

The 1993 trading year

As the end of the first half approached in September, the company had to issue another profits warning – this time via the Announcements Office. Profit forecasts were halved to £18m, the shares fell 63p to 140p, gearing had climbed to 100 per cent and the Chief Executive announced he was retiring early.

When the results were announced further shocks were revealed – losses of £5m, dividend omitted, and increased borrowings to £154m compared with shareholders' funds of £109m. All this pointed to LIG needing to raise cash. Also published was an analysis of the previous comparable half-year figures, showing that they included £3m from a one-off gain on foreign currency holdings and £2m from releasing provisions. These facts were not disclosed at the time and will not have pleased the institutions. More cautious accounting policies would have depressed profits by another £2m. The Chairman, announcing his resignation, said 'LIG was starting a new era'. The photoprocessing division, with a book value of £30m, was to be sold, together with some of the health and beauty brands. The market reaction was to mark the shares down 20 per cent to 111p.

By the end of April 1993 a rights issue was becoming inevitable.

Despite some disposals, cash was flowing out of the business. In these situations further borrowing is not usually a serious option. During May the photoprocessing business was sold. That is if you can regard 'sold' as the right word for a business transferred free of debt and leasing commitments, taking only trade debtors and supplier creditors with a loan of £6m for 18 months, interest-free for the first year.

The year continued unhappily and 9 June was another sorry day in the life of LIG. The full year results to 31 March 1994 revealed a net loss of £174m, including £91m relating to the disposal of the photoprocessing division. Debt was £168m and net assets were £11m negative. A rights issue of 1 for 1 at 70p was proposed, raising £115m. The share price fell to 90p. Disposals were to continue and a new £115m loan was agreed with five banks conditional on the rights issue succeeding. The issue was underwritten by S. G. Warburg and institutional support was encouraging. The rights issue attracted 88.3 per cent acceptances. The remaining 11.7 per cent was purchased at 84p per share by an existing Malaysian investor, taking its stake up to 9.5 per cent. The premium of 14p per share will go to those holders who failed to take up their rights. The issue has strengthened the balance sheet but gearing remains at almost 80 per cent. Consultants have been called in to evaluate the group's brands which could be to prepare and strengthen defences in the event of a possible take-over. The story has not ended yet.

FIELD GROUP PLC

The Field Group illustration involves one of several companies that came to the UK stock market in 1993 following a management buy-out, in this case two years earlier. The timing of the flotation was influenced by the success of earlier offers of similar size companies and the desire of the backers to the management buy-out to realise some of the gains in their investment.

Key case points

- Financing a management buy-out
- Company valuation
- Flotation of a company in the UK market
- Placing and public offer

Background

The Field businesses have been operating for more than 100 years. Starting as a general printer in Bradford, Yorkshire, the business began to specialise in printing folding cartons in the 1920s. It became part of Reed International plc in 1964 and expanded until 1988 when it became the then largest management buy-out in the UK. In July 1990 it was acquired by Svenska Cellulosa Aktiebolaget (SCA). In May 1991 the company became a management buy-out for the second time with 600 employees participating and backing from institutional investors.

Field is a producer of consumer packaging, specialising in the design, manufacture and sale of printed folding cartons. It is the market leader in the UK with a market share of 14.5 per cent and has an expanding presence in Continental Europe. The group has a long-established customer base across a wide range of market sectors including food, tobacco, drinks, confectionery and pharmaceuticals. The branded products for which Field provides packaging include Cadbury's Milk Tray, Chanel, Chivas Regal, Johnnie Walker, Kodak, McVities, Silk Cut and Persil.

The valuation and financing of the 1991 buyout

The value of a company is determined using the financial numbers but also considering market forecasts, production capacity, competitive pricing and long term prospects. In this case, although the company was going to be a separate entity on the open market for the first time, there had already been a market price calculated for the company as a whole only two years before, when the second management buy-out took place. The cost of the buy-out in 1991 was £97.5m, including a subsidiary which had subsequently been sold for almost £20m.

The financing for the buyout was in the following form:

	£m
Issued preference and ordinary share capital including premium (part redeemable)	22.0
Loans raised	30.5
Zero coupon bonds	35.0
	97.5

Zero coupon bonds are loans to a company where cash interest is not paid until the bonds mature. Benefits to the borrower are:

- no cash interest costs are incurred
- interest can be included in the profit statement
- although not paid in cash, the interest counts as a tax deductible expense thus lowering the tax payable and having a direct effect on cash.

They are a particularly suitable method of financing for companies where taxable profits exist but cash is restricted, in such situations as:

- rapidly growing companies where cash is often being absorbed to finance expansion
- short term funding situations such as the interim period between buy-out or venture capital investment and flotation or trade sale.

These bonds had a face value of £50.5m of which £43.5m was payable on 1 April 1994 and £7m on 1 April 1996. Of the £72m raised by the company in July 1993, £48m was needed to repay these bonds, allowing for interest received before payment was made. The timing of the flotation was influenced by this need for cash. The redeemable preference share capital was repurchased at a cost of £21m. This left, after costs, around £2.5m net cash inflow into the business.

The valuation prior to flotation

A decision had to be made on what price at which to offer the shares. Chapter 5 contains details of the techniques that can be applied to produce a valuation. A first step is to examine reported figures. Key figures for the two financial years prior to the Field Group coming to the market were:

Profit statement

		Year ended (£000s)	
		29.03.92	04.04.93
Turnover	– continuing operations	124,453	138,749
	– discontinued operations	7,332	–
		131,785	138,749
Operating costs	– exceptional	(1,000)	(1,953)
	– other	(120,737)	(126,157)
		(121,737)	(128,110)
Operating profit	– continuing operations	9,193	10,639
	– discontinued operations	855	–
		10,048	10,639
Interest payable		(6,058)	(7,262)
Tax payable		(1,682)	(889)
Dividends		(734)	(1,750)
Profit		1,574	738

Interest, tax and dividends relate to the post-buy-out period in the year ended 29.03.92. This period was 45 weeks.

Position statement

		Year ended (£000s)	
		29.03.92	04.04.93
Tangible fixed assets		57,754	62,415
Current assets	– stock	17,735	19,227
	– debtors	23,251	21,706
	– cash	7,959	7,410
		48,945	48,343
Current liabilities	– bank borrowings	(2,059)	(1,240)
(due within one year)	– zero coupon bonds	(38,725)	
	– other	(28,798)	(29,049)
		(30,857)	(69,014)
Net current assets		18,088	(20,671)
Net total assets		75,842	41,744
Longer term liabilities	– bank borrowings	(9,210)	(8,878)
	– zero coupon bonds	(38,714)	(4,944)
		(47,924)	(13,822)
Provisions		(2,781)	(1,804)
		25,137	26,118
Capital and reserves	– issued shares	600	601
	– share premium	20,957	21,034
	– retained profit	2,027	2,930
	– reserves	1,553	1,553
	(mainly subsidiary acquisition related)		
		25,137	26,118

Cash flow statement

	Year ended (£000s)	
	29.03.92	04.04.93
Operating cash flow	20,489	16,878
Net interest paid	(2,132)	(2,158)
Dividends paid	(520)	(1,504)
Taxation	(876)	(1,110)
Investing activities		
Net purchase of tangible fixed assets	(8,580)	(11,733)
The buy-out	(97,565)	–
Buy-out expenses	(2,336)	(558)
Disposal of subsidiary	18,140	1,565
Financing		
Issue of ordinary share capital	23,852	78
Net loan repayments	(20,556)	(2,335)
Buyout loan finance	65,507	–
Increase (decrease) in cash	(4,577)	(877)

The figures extracted to provide valuations would be:

- market value – not available
- asset based – balance sheet   £26m
- earnings based.

Operating profit

Pre-exceptional costs	Post-exceptional costs	Post-interest	Post-Tax
£12.7m	£10.6m	£3.4m	£2.5m

Operating cash flow	Net cash flow
£16.9m	£3.7m

Capitalising the profits and cash flows would produce the following values: using a projected rate of return assumed to be 6 per cent

Operating profit:	pre-exceptional costs	212
	post-exceptional costs	177
	post-interest	57
	post-tax	42
Cash flows:	operating	282
	net	62

The above variations are based on future projections of historic numbers. They ignore entirely intangible assets, such as brands, and the impact of potential future costs such as:

- major costs necessary to maintain the current level of profitability
- cost of compliance with environmental and pollution control legislation
- onerous purchasing or employment contracts.

In many cases these cannot be quantified because even their existence may be uncertain.

Details of the offer

The company was floated successfully in July 1993 with a market capitalisation of £148m. The offer of ordinary shares was a combination of a placing and public offer. Placing is the process of pre-selling shares to selected investors, normally by the merchant bank advising the company. In this case 65 per cent of the shares offered were sold in this way, the balance being offered to the public. The group aimed to raise £84m from the flotation, which would divide as follows:

- £72m to the company from selling almost 30m shares
- £12m to existing shareholders – backers of the buy-out, directors and employees who sold almost 5m shares.

The return to the venture capitalists, valuing their remaining holdings at the share issue price of £2.50, was around 300 per cent in just two years.

The offer was very successful, being over-subscribed 7.4 times, meaning 46,280 investors applied to buy 89.7m shares. The number on

offer to the public was just over 12m. The normal procedure for handling this situation is to allocate fewer shares than applied for, but with
this level of over-subscription it was difficult to do this in economic
quantities. The solution devised was to go into a ballot. The last time in
recent history that this had been necessary was in 1989 when Harry
Ramsden's, the famous Yorkshire-based fish and chip shop, was
floated. The company has prospered since then and boasts outlets at
Heathrow Airport and in Hong Kong, with openings planned in Dublin,
Jeddah and Melbourne in 1995. The type of arrangement Field devised
is typical of those necessary to ensure total allocation of the shares for
sale. The arrangement was:

- applications for 200–500 will go into a ballot for 200 shares
- applications for 750–2,000 will go into a ballot for 400 shares
- applications for 3,000–10,000 will get 13.5 per cent of the amount
  requested
- applications for 15,000–500,000 will get 10 per cent of the amount
  requested
- applications above 500,000 (requiring a cheque for £1.25m with
  application) will get nothing, but the cheque will not be cashed rather
  than refunded after the ballot.

Advantages of flotation

- Created the opportunity for existing shareholders to realise all or part
  of their investments immediately and in the future by open market
  sales.
- Provided an enhanced visibility and greater impression of stability
  which were important for a company having major UK and
  international companies as customers.
- Enabled the group to raise finance more easily in commercial
  markets because of the more public and fuller information
  disclosures required for listed companies.
- Opened up the future possibility of a rights issue by widening the
  shareholder base and encouraging more longer term investors,
  primarily by replacing venture capitalists with institutional
  investors.

The first 'listed' year

Turnover increased by 11 per cent and profit, before exceptional items and tax, increased by 15 per cent to £13.7m. The company acquired the packaging division of the Boots Company in 1993, securing valuable continuing contracts to supply packaging needs. The tone of the Chairman's statement is confident, promising further growth both organically and by acquisition.

EURO DISNEY

Euro Disney was the fourth theme park to be built by the Walt Disney Corporation, famous for its animated films and characters. It follows the incredible success in Florida, California and Tokyo, Japan.

Key case points

- Innovative financing of a major project
- A case of the power of a brand and how it can translate to financial value

Background

The Walt Disney Corporation has been market leader in the entertainment industry for more than 50 years. Following the success of its theme parks in the US it ventured into Japan. The idea of setting up a Disneyland in Europe originated in the 1970s but it was not until 1984 that the project really got going.

The location decision

The first phase of Euro Disney was a Magic Kingdom with 29 attractions, an 18-hole golf course, six hotels with 5,200 rooms and landscaped surroundings with 150,000 trees. The size of the complex and future planned expansion meant that a huge site was needed. Disney felt that developments in the past had not benefited fully from the real estate potential. In Anaheim (California) Disney's land values had risen at 20 per cent a year for 25 years. In Orlando (Florida) the increases had reached 30 per cent and in Tokyo the value of land around the park rose at a faster rate than any land in Japan. Disney's aim was not to repeat the mistake.

The chosen site is at Marne-la-Vallée, 20 miles west of Paris, with 310m people within two hours' flying time. The French Government was very keen to attract Disney to the site. It saw the prospect of between 12,000 and 30,000 jobs being created and tourism revenues of $1bn–$3bn. The package put together to compete with the main rival, Barcelona, was tempting. The land – 4,800 acres in all – was sold by the French Government at 1971 agricultural land prices. Also on offer was an extension of the RER railway line from Paris, new road junctions from the motorway and a link-up with Eurotunnel via the TGV line.

Despite Government enthusiasm, not all the French people were happy to welcome Euro Disney. At the public share issue demonstrators protested, calling it a 'cultural Chernobyl'. At that time the Disney Chairman was quoted as saying his biggest fear was that the park would be too successful and visitors would have to be turned away.

The financing

The Walt Disney Corporation devised an elaborate plan to finance the project. The key approach was to exploit the brand and reputation (known internally as 'the Mouse') by taking on partners and asking them for cash contributions. Here again the French Government was very accommodating. It offered a subordinated loan of $800m at low interest (7.85 per cent) fixed for 20 years. Also allowed was a unique concept – the right of 'accelerated depreciation'. Essentially this permitted Disney to do three things:

- depreciate its fixed assets over 10 rather than 20 years and allow this as a tax deduction. This meant tax deductibility was quicker, thus providing valuable cash flow benefits
- sell these 'rights to future tax deduction' to French investors to reduce their own individual tax bills in the future, in return for immediate cash payments to Disney
- invest the proceeds as equity, thus helping to lower the rates payable on borrowings.

The banks were happy to lend $1.5bn, and European shareholders contributed $900m for 51 per cent of the equity, leaving Disney owning the remaining 49 per cent.

The Disney plan had two other innovative sources of finance. The first was a form of unsecured convertible zero coupon bond called LYONS (Liquid Yield Option Notes) offered in the US. The essential features were:

- an investment of $412 in June 1990
- maturing to $1,000 in June 2005
- equivalent to a yield of 6 per cent (a low rate when compared to 9 per cent on US Treasury Bonds at that time)
- convertible to the $ cash equivalent of 19.7 Euro Disney shares in 2005 (from the 49 per cent of Euro Disney owned by the parent company)
- the up-side was limited. If the value of the investment rose above $619.56 for 20 consecutive days in the two years after issue, Disney could buy back ('call') the bonds, paying only $462.92, including accrued interest of $51 (equivalent to a 6 per cent yield).

As the bonds were zero coupon, Disney had no cash interest payments to make.

The second method was perhaps the cleverest. Disney formed a number of real estate partnerships with service providers such as fast-food outlets. Their normal arrangement would be to pay a percentage of their sales and a rental payment for buildings and facilities. Disney added another aspect to this, asking the service provider to build and pay for its own outlet. This was helpful in reducing development costs for Disney. Even more helpful was the agreement that the outlet 'owner' would then give the building to Disney, allowing it to do a 'sale and leaseback' to banks. Disney walked away with $400m from these deals and the lease payments were to be made out of the sales commissions received.

The trading arrangements

Although Disney owns only 49 per cent of the equity, the management of the park is under the control of a limited partnership. As Disney is the general partner it retains full operational control of the park and any land development around it. Thus full control is achieved with a minority holding. Disney, as the owner of the brand and concept, receives royalties from its use. These are considerable:

- merchandise and hotels revenues 7 per cent
- admission revenues 5 per cent
- dividends of 49 per cent of net income.

The real bonanza is the management fee structure:

- base fee 3 per cent of revenues for the first five years
- After five years this goes up to 6 per cent

A final reward comes from the cash flow performance:

- if operating cash flow hits $220m, Disney's take is 30 per cent.
- above $450m it goes up to half of the cash flow.

The recent picture

The attendances have not been high, and those who have visited did not spend. Losses are being incurred and painful refinancing has been necessary. Disney has waived its right to royalties and management fees for five years and the banks have accepted an 18-month interest holiday on their loans.

The main disappointment for Disney is not the income – it produced only $36m of the total $1.7bn operating income last year – but rather the prospect of enormous real estate gains from land and, particularly, hotels. The then CFO of Disney had come from Marriott Hotels and he saw the potential for sale and leaseback deals. If these ever happen Disney will really reap the benefit of its European investment.

The shareholders have little to be happy about. The value of their investment is declining and any prospect of dividend is a fairy story worthy of Disney itself. Perhaps this tale of fantasy says it all:

> ONCE UPON A TIME, in a large field of sugar beet near the city of Paris, a Very Rich Man told everyone that he would build Europe's biggest theme park. Nearly everyone laughed and told him he was mad. 'Lend me lots of money and, honestly, this park will make you all rich,' he said.
>
> 'Perhaps he's right,' said some of Paris's important people, 'We do need jobs, after all.' The Very Rich Man said that if they didn't give him the money he would take his park to Spain or Britain. The people were frightened, so they handed over money. The park was built and, as the Very Rich Man had promised, visitors came. But not enough visitors for the Very Rich Man to repay the Very Large Debts. He turned again to the local people, 'Help me. Lend me more money and everything will turn out well.' The local people became very angry because they saw they had been very foolish: 'You are a Very Rich Man. Why should we lend you more money? In fact, come to think of it, as you are Very Rich, how come we lent you so much money in the first place?'

© *The Independent* 24.02.94

EURO DISNEY - SOURCES OF FINANCE

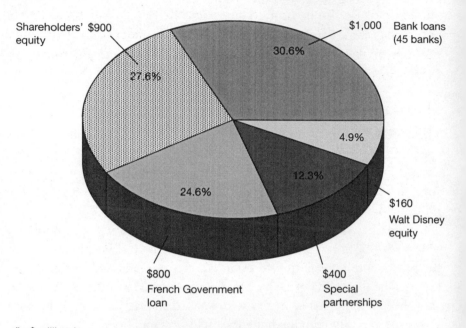

Shareholders' $900 equity

27.6%

$1,000   Bank loans (45 banks)

30.6%

4.9%

12.3%

24.6%

$160 Walt Disney equity

$800 French Government loan

$400 Special partnerships

(in $ millions)

Figure 11.2

ALLIED LYONS PLC

Allied Lyons plc is a major UK food and drinks group and had a turnover of £4.7bn in 1990, rising modestly to £5.5b in 1994. Its pretax profits were £565m in 1990 and have been under pressure, rising to £606m in 1994. The group acquired the Pedro Domecq spirits and sherry business in 1994.

Key case points

- Use of currency management techniques and instruments
- The line between protection and speculation in currency management
- Treasury as a profit centre or cost centre
- The pitfalls of forecasting

Background

The company which became Allied Lyons was formed in the 1960s from a merger of brewery companies. It expanded through the 1920s into spirits, wine and food with the acquisition of the J. Lyons Company, becoming Allied Lyons in 1981. It is now focused on four business areas:

- spirits and wine –   Ballantines Scotch
                            Courvoisier Brandy
                            Beefeater Gin
                            Domecq Sherry
- retailing –   Dunkin Donuts
                            Baskin Robbins Ice Cream
                            Victoria Wine Off-licences
- brewing and wholesaling – Carlsberg
                            Tetley Bitter
                            Skol
- food manufacturing –   Tetley Tea
                            Maryland Cookies.

The crisis

The company hit the headlines on 20 March 1991 with a report of a £150m loss on foreign exchange dealing, the resignation of the Finance Director and the launch of an investigation by the auditors. The share price dropped 32p on the day to 517p, reflecting how the market viewed the biggest loss ever by a UK industrial company in 'abnormal foreign exchange exposures'.

The root cause of the loss can be traced back to 1989 when the company treasury team decided to start selling (writing) call options on foreign currencies which gave the buyer the right (but not the obligation) to obtain that currency at a fixed exchange rate. If the market moves in the predicted direction the option fee is pure profit to the seller. Sadly, if the market moves the opposite way the seller has potentially unlimited exposure.

It is standard practice for companies, particularly those with a large element of dollar-based income, to hedge against adverse currency movements. The transactions at Allied Lyons were way beyond protecting anything that arose from ordinary trading. By the end of the second half of 1990 the company's exposure limit of £500m had been breached. Although the treasury was not officially classified as a profit centre, it had made modest profits in the past – £3m in 1988, £5m in 1989 and £9m in 1990.

Mainly because the writing of options was a profitable business the team became increasingly aggressive, taking ever greater risks. Whether this was an attempt to make a bottom-line difference to compensate for a slow-down in operations will probably never be known. It was unfortunate that this change in operation was not detected within the business because computer systems were outdated, internal controls were not strictly enforced and perhaps the full extent of the risks being taken on was not understood by staff.

Although senior management had received several warnings during 1990 of the increased involvement of the company in foreign exchange markets it was only in September that the treasury team began to reduce the exposure to more prudent levels. Between 21 February and 16 March 1991 the dollar strengthened considerably from $1.96 to $1.79. This left Allied Lyons in an unhedged short position, meaning that the company had promised to deliver dollars for pounds at a rate that was now more than 8 per cent the wrong way – and growing. When the Natwest Bank was called in to 'close out the positions' on Monday 18 March it had to buy $1bn to meet the commitments, creating a loss close to $150m in the process. It is a sad irony that this trade in itself, being unusually large, contributed to further strengthening of the dollar.

Although it is unlikely that Allied will write any more options, it did at least retain its independence, unlike J. Lyons (the 'Lyons' in Allied Lyons) which when acquired in the 1970s had problems that followed very expensive Swiss Franc borrowing.

SPRING RAM PLC

Spring Ram plc was a much praised story of dynamic business development using high technology plant to produce a range of sanitary fittings, furniture and accessories for the do-it-yourself market.

Key case points

- Accounting policies
- Investor and City relations
- Corporate Governance
- The effects of poor internal financial control

Background

From its beginnings in 1979 this Yorkshire-based business became one of the outstanding success stories of the 1980s in the UK. As a manufacturer of kitchen and bathrooom furniture and accessories, primarily for the do-it-yourself market, it prospered in line with the growth in housing development and values. Its sales grew to £194.2m in 1991 with pre-tax profits of £37.6m. The company operated from state-of-the-art factories on greenfield sites in northern England.

Business development

Spring Ram's ability to generate cash to support its capital expenditure meant no long term borrowings. In fact, in 1990, interest on cash in the business contributed £2.2m to profits. The only criticisms of the 1991 performance in the City were slight doubts about 'the miserly depreciation charge' and the high stock levels. The response was blunt: 'We build for stock'. The company cited also its reputation for prompt delivery. The lack of gearing indicated that it could afford the policy anyway. The first half of 1992 saw further advances in profits, but as the company got bigger the scrutiny of the accounts got tougher. The highly rated stock – it was floated in 1983 with a market value of £11m, rising to a peak of £650m in May 1992 – also attracted media attention.

The crisis

Late 1992 saw the company's share price fall by a third as concern about internal financial controls grew following an announcement of unanticipated exceptional charges of £5.6m to cover 'serious misrepresentation and false accounting' at a subsidiary. The announcement was accompanied by the news of an agreed takeover of Stag Furniture Holdings. The company's stockbroker insisted on the announcement as soon as it was informed of the problem. The company had delayed, as legal advice supported the view that it could wait until the 'full scale of the problem' was known. One analyst put it more unkindly – 'naïvety or a cock-up'. The Finance Director attempted to allay criticism by issuing a request that 'this isolated incident should not undermine people's confidence in our ability to run the business'. The fact is that the subsidiary could have been better controlled, and when the problem was revealed to be larger than expected the management were silent – not the way to make friends in the financial comunity.

A later statement by the Finance Director spelled out three distinct areas of false accounting: the value of closing stock was inflated to increase the gross profit, the quantity of items in stock was overstated and sales were effectively inflated by ignoring returns from distributors. The subsidiary Finance Director was dismissed, but the composition of the main board came under scrutiny. With media attention on the Cadbury report on Corporate Governance, the total absence of non-executive directors was noted.

Board changes

In July 1993 a new Finance Director was appointed and an executive Chairman brought in by the institutional shareholders. The Chief Executive, and holder of 16 per cent of the voting shares, remained. By September he and all the previous executive directors had departed.

1993 results

The results for that year were not catastrophic. Changes in accounting policy had resulted in profit reductions and some asset write-downs.

Shareholders' funds had fallen from £130m to £89m, but the Chairman was confident about prospects for 1994, with turnover increasing in all divisions.

Rights issue

Early 1994 saw the announcement of a 2 for 9 rights issue price at 53p per new ordinary, designed to raise £42m and strengthen the balance sheet by reducing bank borrowings. It was hoped this would also enable strategic development and finance increased trading opportunities. A token dividend was announced together with an intention to pursue a progressive dividend policy with an appropriate level of cover.

Developments during 1994

The cash and trading positions were described as satisfactory, with some cause for optimism. An acquisition of a bed manufacturing company, Rest Assured, was completed mid-year at a cost of £5m. It is hoped that Rest Assured will turn into profit shortly, after reporting a first quarter 1994 loss.

SAATCHI AND SAATCHI

Saatchi and Saatchi was one of the fastest-growing UK companies of the 1980s. Starting from a small advertising agency in 1970 it became the world's tenth largest consulting firm in the late 1980s. It had a long list of high-profile clients, including British Airways, the Conservative Party, American Express, 3M and Mars.

Key case points

- Acquisition valuations with substantial intangible assets
- Financial rescue package
- Issue of convertible shares

Background

Saatchi and Saatchi had grown dramatically in the 1980s, mainly by acquisition, from a small advertising agency to a global provider of consultancy services – a one-stop shop. It was dominated by the founders, the Saatchi brothers, Maurice and Charles, whose ambition was to create a business that would be in the top five in each of its activities in all of the world's major markets. At its height, in 1987, as part of its expansion into financial services it even proposed a merger with the Midland Bank, at that time almost double Saatchi and Saatchi's own size.

Financing the expansion

Saatchi had financed its expansion by using almost every source – rights issues, convertibles and borrowings – with alarming frequency. A typical illustration is the issue in June 1987 of 6.75 per cent redeemable convertible preference shares 2003 of £1 each. These shares can be converted between October 1989 and July 2003 at 44p per share. At the time, the shares were around 360p and the issue relied upon the climate of rising share prices in setting the conversion terms. Had all the conversions taken place it would have increased the number of ordinary shares by 22 per cent. The shares had a 'put option' giving holders the right to sell the shares back to the company. In this case

Saatchi could have been required to pay £211m in July 1993 to the holders. This was an attractive risk-reduction element, enabling the company to borrow at a lower rate. Saatchi thought it would never be repaid as the conversion to ordinary shares would be so attractive. This did not work out to be the scenario. By the end of 1990 the share price was down to 37p having peaked at nearly 700p in 1986. The first opportunity for the preference shareholders to demand repayment was coming up in July 1993.

At current share price levels then, the £212m needed was three times the market capitalisation of the company. Any thought of selling assets to raise the cash required a high degree of optimism. The cash had been used for acquisition of advertising agencies and consultancy practices. This type of business is long on intangible people assets, short on tangible fixed assets. As global markets had turned down, profitability and cash generation had worsened and the prices paid looked high.

The existence of the put option gave the convertible owners a stranglehold on the company. Plainly, the need to pay £212m would lead to bankruptcy. The price of avoiding this would have to be heavy dilution for existing ordinary shareholders, and no prospect of dividends for some years.

The rescue package

Early in 1991 proposals were made by the new Chief Executive, Robert Louis-Dreyfus, to refinance the company. The key features were:

- a rights issue to raise £55m at a share price of 10p
- an offer to the management to sell shares, raising £4m personally underwritten by Mr Dreyfus
- an offer by Mr Dreyfus to subscribe for £1m of shares
- existing ordinary shareholders would see their holding diluted to 17 per cent of what it was before
- repayment of the company's £200m debt would be deferred from January 1993 to January 1996.

The refinancing was completed in April 1991, providing at least a breathing space.

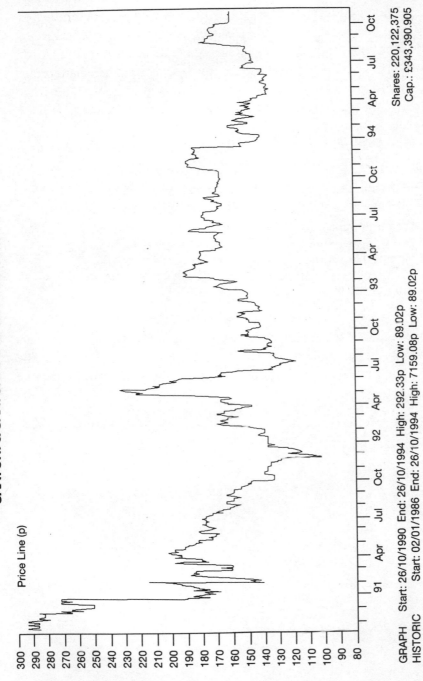

SAATCHI & SAATCHI COMPANY PLC ORD 25P

Price Line (p)

GRAPH   Start: 26/10/1990 End: 26/10/1994 High: 292.33p Low: 89.02p
HISTORIC Start: 02/01/1986 End: 26/10/1994 High: 7159.08p Low: 89.02p

Shares: 220,122,375
Cap.: £343,390.905

Figure 11.3

The 1991 results

To quote the Chairman, 'The results were poor'. Revenue was down, margins were down and losses were almost £60m. Cash flow was negative. The impact of changes in accounting policy led to a restatement of the 1990 extraordinary items to £264m, reflecting goodwill write-offs.

The 1992 results

To quote the Chairman again, 'The results are still far from satisfactory'. Revenue increased slightly and there was a small profit before the policy on accounting for goodwill on acquisition was reviewed. This led to a £60m write-off in the profit and loss account. Debt remained at over £200m.

The 1993 results

The 1993 trading year brought the company back to modest profitability, but the share price has yet to recover to its levels of two years previously. The equivalent would be 175p – the price after the results announcement was 140p. The graph shows the adjusted price movements.

METALLGESELLSCHAFT

Metallgesellschaft is a mining metals and industrial group based in Frankfurt with 250 subsidiaries worldwide. It was in the top 20 largest German companies in 1993, with a turnover of Dm27bn. Its key expansion aim was to become the biggest provider of environmental services in Europe, specialising in recycling, pollution control and decontamination processes.

Key case points

- German corporate governance
- Use of financial derivatives
- Accounting policies

Background

Metallgesellschaft was an acclaimed example of a German company demonstrating the benefits of Germany's system of corporate governance. It had been led for five years by Heinz Schimmelbusch, who was voted German manager of the Year in 1991. Although the company was suffering from low price competition with the Eastern bloc and the severity of the German recession, who better to run the company in 1992 but the reigning Manager of the Year?

The profit in 1991–2 was reported as Dm245m, but the failure of the company to adopt the standard formula used by most large German companies to smooth the effects of one-off extraordinary and exceptional income raised suspicions in the international investment community. Specific gains were left buried within an overall profit figure.

Current situation

The year ended September 1993 presented a rather different picture. Turnover remained static at Dm25.5bn, but profits had disappeared, leaving a loss of Dm347m. The share price halved in two weeks during December 1993 after a US subsidiary, MG Corporation, hit liquidity problems. The cause was the need to meet 'margin calls' – cash payments relating to future contracts. The total loss was Dm3.2bn, bringing Metallgesellschaft perilously close to bankruptcy. The need to make extra payments arose out of the fall in oil prices during 1993. In May a barrel cost $21, by December, after a rapid fall at the end of November, the price was $14.

The impact of the crisis

The career of Herr Schimmelbusch came to an end abruptly on 20 December 1993 when he was fired, together with his Finance Director. The reason given for his departure was his failure to keep the supervisory board informed of the problems with the group's US subsidiary. Four further directors were elbowed out – two retired, two demoted.

German corporate governance

The German system of corporate governance has been quoted as one of the ingredients for the success of the post-war German economy. The co-operation between banks, government and labour seemed to offer an encouraging environment for long term planning. Companies have a low dependence on stock market finance as their main source of finance. Founding families often retain large holdings, and direct investment by banks and insurance companies is very significant. Metallgesellschaft was typical of this: Deutsche Bank, Dresdner Bank and the Allianz Insurance Group together owned 26 per cent of the shares.

The ultimate power in a German company is vested with the supervisory board, which consists of representatives of shareholders and employees in equal measure, with the Chairman having the casting vote. The Chairman in this case was a board member of Deutsche Bank. Day to day control is exercised by the management board, reporting to the supervisory board. The advantage of this structure is the protection it gives to the company from the need to pay attention to short term stock market fluctuations and ultimately from the threat of hostile takeover bids. The drawback is that if supervisory boards get too close to management they fail to act as a 'check', but shield the company from the discipline of a public financial market.

The final outcome

On 6 January 1994 Metallgesellschaft stunned the market when it announced revised losses for last year of Dm2bn, up from Dm347m, requested a huge injection of funds and proposed the conversion of Dm1.3bn of debt to convertible stock. The board also requested Dm500m in new lines of credit, in addition to the Dm1.5bn granted in December 1993, and a 90-day debt moratorium. Also announced were asset sales, cuts in the workforce and future further potential losses of Dm1bn in the next two or three years caused by continuing problems in the US subsidiary.

The revised loss exceeded shareholders' funds, and without support from bank lenders the unthinkable prospect of the fourteenth largest German company going into liquidation was a real possibility. The financial community joined together and backed the company. The reaction of one Frankfurt-based banker summed up the feelings of the banking community the day after: 'It was a bit like waking up after a car crash and finding you could still move your arms and legs.' In other words, it could have been worse. Meanwhile the former Chief Executive and Finance Director were being formally investigated on suspicion of fraud and failure to inform the supervisory board of developments.

On 11 January 1994 the amount of new credit requested was increased to Dm700m without a detailed explanation. This caused one banker to criticise the way the rescue package was presented as an 'all or nothing, take it or leave it' ultimatum. On 14 January, trading in Metallgesellschaft shares was suspended, pending changes in the rescue package. The main change was halving the request for new credit to Dm350m. Agreement was reached on 16 January, with the result that the German banks, notably Deutsche Bank and Dresdner Bank, putting in more cash and foreign-owned banks less.

There was need for haste. Under German bankruptcy law the supervisory board would have had to declare bankruptcy within 21 days of it becoming clear that the company had negative net assets. This meant the latest date for agreement was 25 January – earlier if the supervisory board was informed before the public announcement. By 14 May the storm appeared to be over. Disposals were ongoing, cost cutting measures planned, inventory levels reduced and investment curtailed. The share price had recovered strongly on this news, up by 25 per cent in a week to Dm280.

A week is a long time in business and by 26 May the shares had fallen back to Dm220 following the disclosure of the need to make extra provisions to cover newly identified risks arising from oil operations in North America. By late June, following further disposals, the headquarters site in the centre of Frankfurt went up for sale. The Chief Executive warned on 22 June that the US subsidiary was still a 'machine for losing money'. Contracts entered into with the Castle Corporation, a 40 per cent owned associate, were described as 'inexplicable'. These contracts forced MG Corporation to supply Castle with crude oil and finance the purchases. MG then had to buy back the oil at *above the market price until the year 2000*. Metallgesellschaft had total debts at the end of March 1994 of Dm9bn. The final chapter in this saga has yet to come.

INDEX

hedging, currency risk 130
hire purchase 39

IBCA 37–9
IBM 74
Icahn, Carl 19
income statements, *see* profit and loss
statements
inflation 59, 73
information sources 6–11, 84–7
Initial Public Offerings (IPOs) 19
Institutional Investors Committee 19
intangibles 73–6, 85–6
intellectual property 74–5
Interbrand Group plc 74, 85–6
Internal Rate of Return (IRR) 50–3
IPO (Initial Public Offerings) 19
IRR (Internal Rate of Return) 50–3

Japan Tobacco 23
joint ventures 66

Lamont, Norman 35
lawyers 21
leasing 39–41
Leverhulme, Lord 135
limited companies ix
loan stock 31–2
loans, term 30–1, 33–5
London International Group 25
case study 168–72
London Weekend Television plc, case
study 159–67

McGraw Hill 37
Major, John 35
management
of cash 98–9
of creditors 99–100
of debtors 94–7
of stock 93–4
of working capital 91–3
marginal cost pricing 107–8
Mercedes-Benz 28
merchant banks 21
merger accounting 81–3
mergers 67–8
Metallgesellschaft 120